THIS DAY IN SPORTS HISTORY

Ray G. Claveran

authorHOUSE®

AuthorHouse™
1663 Liberty Drive
Bloomington, IN 47403
www.authorhouse.com
Phone: 1 (800) 839-8640

Published by AuthorHouse 03/13/2019

ISBN: 978-1-7283-0056-6 (sc)
ISBN: 978-1-7283-0057-3 (hc)
ISBN: 978-1-7283-0058-0 (e)

Library of Congress Control Number: 2019901824

Print information available on the last page.

This book is printed on acid-free paper.

DEDICATION

To my wife Aline; thank you for your support and your love. It's been fun writing this book. And isn't that what life is all about. I would also like to thank my three sons Derek, Troy and Ray for their help and support, and thanks to my wife's family and my family and all my friends that I love and mean so much to me.

I was born at night; but it wasn't last night; so I have learned that without support, love, and understanding from Family and good friends I could not or would not have written this book.

ACKNOWLEDGMENT

To me writing this book has been a labor of love, plus I feel that everything I have accomplished in my life I owe to my family my friends and to sports. Thanks to all the coaches I had as a young 10-15 year old kid. And a special thanks to my friends and high school basketball Coach Carl Peregoy and to my community college Basketball and Golf coach Frank Boyle. After leaving school, and for years to follow both of these men became my close personal friends.

I was a very lucky young kid because I know for sure that without the role models I had, there is no telling what I would have done with my life. Men like Ralph Pop Ransom that started me in golf—Mike De Massey that hired me as his Assistant at Elkhorn Golf and Country Club IN Stockton California. Today I am a life member of the PGA of America, thanks to my coaches that taught me Most of what I have learned about sports. Good men that taught me how to win Fair and how to lose with dignity.

INTRODUCTION

FROM A FANS STANDPOINT

I have been an avid sports fan since the 1950's.Prior to the 60's I played high school and 2 years of college basketball and was on the college golf team Today I am a Life Member of the PGA of America. So I can say that I have had a love affair with Sports. I truly believe that true honest and fair competition in sports builds character.

To compete in any sporting event and to win fair and square is something to be proud of, if you did not win fairly then there is nothing to be proud of. If you did not win fairly you did not win you lost. You should never accept first place if you know it belongs to another.

I firmly believe that if a young boy plays team sports, and is well coached, not only about the particular sport he is involved in but also the importance of the rules, and fair play, this will contribute to building character. Playing team sports a young boy will develop friendships that will last a lifetime. Sports will help a young man learn about loyalty and how to work together as a unit. Sports can also teach a young man about adversity and how to accept defeat

A young man learns that winning is the reward for all the hard work in the past, the harder you work at practice—the luckier you get in the game.

Personally I have the utmost respect for Professional athletes, especially those that take the responsibility to be good role models for young boys and girls.

TABLE OF CONTENTS

● ● ● ● ● ● ● ● ● ● ● ● ● ● ● ● ● ●

CHAPTER 1

ON THIS DAY IN SPORTS HISTORY-(BASEBALL)

In 1936 five of the greatest players in Major league history were inducted into The Baseball Hall of Fame at the same time; the five inductees were Babe Ruth—Walter Johnson—Honus Wagner—Christy Mathewson—and Ty Cobb

On this day in Sports History, January 22, 2019 The voting tabulations were anounced tuesday by Hall of Fame President Jeff Idelson. Mariano Rivera, Roy Halladay, Edgar Mrtinez, and Mike Mussina will be inducted in Cooperstown on July21,2019

Mariano Rivera will be the first unanimous selaction in Major league baseball history, He received 100% of the 425 votes. Halladay and Martinez both got 85.4% of the votes,(363 vots) and Mike Mussina 326 votes which was 76.7%.

On this day in Sports History January 5,1920 the Boston Red Sox sold pitcher, outfielder Babe Ruth to the New York Yankees for 125,000 Dollars This Sale later became know as the Curse of the Bambino and would haunt the Red Sox for years that followed.

On this day in Sports History, September 27, 2018 Colorrado Pockies Right handed pitcher German Marquez tied the modern day major league record when he had eight straight strikeouts against Philadelphia to start a ball game.The record was held by Houston lefty Jim Deshies on september 23, 1986, and New York Mets right hand pitcher Jacob de Grom September 15,2014

On this day in Sports History, October, 26 2018 in the third game, the Los Angelese Dodger's Max Muncy hit an 18th inning walk off homer to beat the Boston Red Soxin the longest game in World Series History

On this day in Sports History October 28, 2018 The Boston Red Sox Beat the Los Algeles Dodgers in Game five 5 to to win the 2018 World Series.

In Game 1 Boston won by the score of 8–4
In game 2 Boston won 4—2
In game 3 L.a. won 3—2
In game 4 Boston won 9—6
And in game 5 Boston won 5—1

Steve Pearce of the Boston Red Soxwas name the MVP of the 2018 World Series…

The 2018 Rookies of the year in the major leagues

The rookie of the year in the Amrican league was Shohel Ohtani from the Las Angeles Angels. Ohtani was a standout Pitcher and at the plate as well. He hit 10 home runs and had had 4 wins on the Mound.

The rookie of the year in the national league was Ronald Acuna from the Atlanta Braves. Acuna is a 20 year old outfielder.

On this day in Sports History, November 16,1987George Bell Playing for the T0ronto Blue Jays was named the MVP of the American League. Bell was the first player from the Blue Jays to win the Award.

Most valuable players In the major from 2006to 2018American league

(2018—Mookie betts—(Boston
2017— Jose Altuve—Houston
2016—Mike Trout—Los Angeles
2015—Josh Donaldson—Toronto
2014—Mike Trout—Los Angelese
2013—Miguel Cabrera—Detroit
2012—Miguel Cabrera—Detroit
2011—Justin Verlander—Detroit
2010—Josh Hamilton—Texas
2009—Joe Mauer—Minnesota
2008—Dustin Pedroia—Boston
2007—Alex Rodriguez—New York
2006—Justin Morneau—Minnesota

National League

2018-- Christian Yelich—Milwaukee
2017—Giancarlo Stanton—Miami
2016—Kris Bryant—Chicago
2015—Bryce Harper—Washinton
2014—Clayton Kershaw—Los Angeles
2013—Andrew McCutchen—Pittsburgh
2012—Buster Posey—San Francisco
2011—Ryan Braun—Milwaukee
2010—Joey Votto—Cincinnati
2009—Alber Pujols—St Louis
2008—Albert Pujols—St Louis
2007—Jimmy Rollins—Philadelphia
2006—Ryan Howard—Philadelphia

On this day in Sports History, August,30, 1905 Ty Cobb the great Outfielder for the Detroit Tigers made his debut and hit a double on his first time at bat.

On this day in Sports History, August 12, 1951, Eddie Gaedel, who was only 3 feet 7 inches tall made Baseball history by being the first player with dwarfism to play in a Major League Baseball Game. Gaedel had been secretly signed by Bill Veek, the owner of the Browns. Eddie Gaedel wore the number 1/8 on his jersey. He came in as a pinch hitter in the bottom of the first inning in the second game of a double header between the St. Louis Browns and the Detroit Tigers. He was instructed by Bill Veek, not to swing at the ball and he was walked on four straight balls by the pitcher Bob Coin of the Tigers, who couldn't throw low enough to find the strike zone. (Now that is funny stuff)

On this day in Sports History August 26,1939, The first televised major league baseball games were televised on an experimental T. V. station W2XBS. The games were a double header between the Cincinnati Reds and the Brooklyn Dodgers; The Reds won the first game 5-2 and the Brooklyn Dodgers won the second game 6-1 The games were played at Ebbets Field.

On this Day in Sorts History, September 24, 1934 Babe Ruth made his last appearance as a regular player for the Yankees against the Boston Red Sox. The Red Sox won the game 5-0

The last game was played at Yankee Stadium at the end of the 2008 season. Jose Molina hit a homer in the fourth inning, which turned out to be the last hit in the 85 year old stadium. The Yankees won the game over Baltimore 7-3

On this day in Sports History, July 13, 1982, the All-Star game for Major League Baseball was played outside the United States for the First time. The game was played at the Olympic Stadium in Montreal Canada.

On this day in Sports History—August 30, 1912 Earl Hamilton records the first No Hitter in franchise history for the St. Louis Browns against the Detroit Tigers. The Browns won the game 5-1The lone Tiger run came when Ty Cobb got a walk and turned it into a run after an error. The St Louis Browns is the franchise we know today as the Baltimore Orioles..

On this day in Sports History September 9 1954, Dick Fowler pitching for the Philadelphia Athletics became the first and only Canadian to pitch a major league no hitter. Philadelphia won the game1-0

On this day in Sports History— September 8, 1939, Bob Feller, of the Cleveland Indians became the youngest pitcher in major league baseball history to win 20 games in a season. He was 20 years 10 months and 5 days. He entered the record books in front of 598 fans against St, He won the game 12-1 by allowing just 5 hits. Feller ended the season 24-9 and went on to win 20 games six times in his career

On this day in Sports History November 13 2003, Eric Gagne of the Los Angeles Dodgers was named the Cy Young Award winner for the National league, He became the second Canadian to win the award.

On this day in Sports History April 16, 1941; Bob Feller, pitcher for the Cleveland Indians pitched the only Opening day no hitter in Baseball history. Cleveland won the game 1-0 over the Chicago White Sox

On this day In Sports History March 5, 1904; Cy Young Pitched The American League's first perfect game. Young was pitching for the Boston Americans, now the Boston Red Sox,, He won the game 3-0 over the Philadelphia Athletics.

In the 1931 season Lefty Grove Pitching for the Philadelphia Athletics won 31 games in the American league, he was named the American leagues MVP.

On this day in Sports History— September 22, 1911 Cy Young wins number 511against the Pirates, He played for the Boston Rustlers and he was 44 years old at the time. No Pitcher will ever come close to that number again. He holds the record for the most complete games—749 Innings pitched 7,356—Career starts—815 Most consecutive innings pitched without a hit—25and a third innings in 1904Cy Young won the First World Series ever played in, 1903 as a member of the Boston Americans; Now the Boston Red Sox, He also holds the distinction of being the first man to throw the first pitch in a World Series Game. Because of his accomplishments as a pitcher he holds the honor of having the award that is presented to the best pitcher in both leagues EVERY YEAR bear his name; THE CY YOUNG AWARD.

Cy Young was inducted into the Baseball Hall of Fame in 1937

On this day in Sports History June 8, 1982, Satchel Paige Passed away at the age of 42. After Jackie Robinson broke the color barrier Satchel Paige signed a Major league contract to pitch in the American League. Satchel Paige was a great pitcher that played in the Negro league. Prior to signing a rookie contract to play in the Majors Satchel Paige played in the Negro League.

On this day in Sports History, August 5 1952, Satchel Page became the oldest pitcher to pitch a complete game in major league history. He pitched 12 innings and shut-out the Detroit Tigers and beat Virgil Trucks 1-0

On this day in sports history, August 22, 1965, In the third inning when the Giants pitcher, Juan Marichal came to the plate, the great pitcher for the L. A. dodgers, Sandy Koufax was on the mound. Earlier in the game Juan Marichal had brushed back two of the Dodgers batters. When the catcher for the Dodgers, John Roseboro's return throw back to Koufax came too close to Marichal's ear, the confrontation started. Juan Marichal with the bat sill in hands he hit John Roseboro two times on the head. Roseboro required 14 stitches to close the wound. Juan Marichal was fined and suspended for eight games for the incident.

On this day in sports history August 17, 1989, The San Francisco Giants and the Oakland A's were getting ready for game 3 of the Worlds Series at Candlestick Park. Just minutes from the start of the game a magnitude 6.9 Earthquake shook the San Francisco Bay Area causing massive damage to Roads, Bridges and buildings in the Bay area The World

Series was delayed for 10 days so repairs could be made to the damage to Candlestick Park. (Through out the years I have probably watched the San Francisco Giants and the 49ers ballgames at Candlestick at least 100 times—(Mostly from the Stadium Club--they sell beer there.) Candlestick Park was originally built for the Giants, which played their first game there on April 12th, 1960The San Francisco 49ers played their games there from 1971—2013

On this day in Sports History, April 15, Jackie Robinson became the first Black Player to play in the Major Leagues. To my way of thinking Jackie Robinson became one of the most exciting Players to ever play Baseball

In 1947 in his rookie season Jackie Robinson stole home for the first time, He stole home a total of 19 times in his career.

On this day in Sports History, September 17, 1947 Jackie Robinson was named Rookie of the year Robinson signed with the Brooklyn Dodgers and he broke the color barrier in Major League Baseball when he started at first base earlier that year. Robinson was inducted into the Major League Baseball Hall of Fame the very first year he was eligible In 1947 Robinson was bestowed the greatest honor, I believe, any athlete in any sport could receive ; The commissioner of baseball, Bud Selig, officially retired Jackie's jersey number 42for all teams in the Major Leagues

On this day in Sports History, November 10th, 2004 Houston Astros Pitcher Roger Clements was the first pitcher in baseball history in the majors to win the Cy Young Award for the seventh time, He was 42 at the Time which made him the oldest pitcher to win the award, Clements finished the season with 18 wins and just 4 losses. He was named the starting pitcher for the national league in the All Star Team.

On this day in Sports History August 1, 1994 the Major League baseball season was suspended due to the players going on strike. The season ended and there were no post season games, this included the World Series

On this day in Sports History, July 21, 1991, Ferguson Jenkins, born in Chatham Ontario, became the first Canadian to be inducted into Major Leagues Baseball Hall of Fame in Cooperstown New York

On this day in Sports History, May 3, 1980, Ferguson Jenkins became the 4th Pitcher to win 100 games in both the National league and the American league.

On this day in Sports History October 30, 1974 Nolan Ryan throws the fastest pitch ever recorded, he threw a pitch 100.9 Miles per hour!!!

On this day in Sports History September 22, 1993 Nolan Ryan at the age of 46while pitching against the Seattle Mariners in the first inning had to leave the game after tearing an elbow ligament. That injury ended Nolan Ryan's spectacular career. Ryan ended his career as the 20th pitcher to win 300 games. His fast ball has been clocked at over 100 mph. He set the record of of no hitter, he had 7. He set the record of 5,714 Strike Outs, Nolan Ryan had his number was retired by three different teams Nolan Ryan was inducted into the Major League Hall of Fame in 1999

On this day in Sports History, August 5, 1979 Pete Rose of the Philadelphia Phillies Hit his 2,427 base hit to break the record that was held by Honus Wagner for years..

)n this day in Sports History April 23, 1954 Hank Aaron hit the first of his 755 home runs Aaron playing for the Milwaukee Braves, later they became the Atlanta Braves, The Braves were playing against the St. Louis Cardinals.

On this day in Sports History June 5 2011 Roberto Alomar was scheduled for induction into the Baseball Hall of Fame. Roberto helped the Toronto Blue Jays win the World Series in 1992 and 1993 Roberto Alomar has the Distinction of being the first Toronto Blue Jay to be inducted into The Hall Of Fame in Cooperstown N.Y.

On this day in Sports History August7th 2007 Barry Bonds hit home run Number 756 to break Hank Aaron home run record. Babe Ruth Had 714—Hank Aaron had 755. Just think these three players had a total of—just a few minutes need my adding machine—2,225

On this day in Sports History, September 8, 1998, Mark McGuire Broke Roger Maris's single season home-run record. McGuire hit his 62nd home run in the fourth inning against the Chicago Cubs He was cheered by the Fans his Team mates and the opposing players as well. When he crossed home plate his son was there to greet him as he was serving as bat boy for the game. —and how nice is that?

On this day in Sports History January11, 2010, Mark Mcguire Admitted that he had used steroids for 10 years, including The year he hit 70 Home-runs in 1998

On this day in Sports History, September 6, 1995 Cal Ripken Jr. the great shortstop for the Baltimore Orioles broke Yankee great lou Gehrigs iron man record by playing in his 213th straight game, Ripken extended the record to 2,632 straight games before sitting out a game against the Yankees on September 21,1998. (hell; I'm tired just thinking about the streak) I

On this day in Sports History, August 23,1982, Gaylord Perry, one of the great pitchers in Baseball was finally caught throwing his famous spitball It was pretty well known or should I say suspected that he threw the spitball for years. At One point it was rumored that he approached Vaseline about endorsing their product.

On this day in Sports History, October 25, 1981Rick Monday of the Los Angeles Dodgers hit a Two out ninth inning home run off Expo pitcher Steve Rogers to beat the Montreal Expos, and give the Dodgers the National League Championship Series. The Expos had defeated the Philadelphia Phillies to win the National League Eastern division title before losing to the Dodgers that fateful day at Olympic Stadium in Toronto. The Epos reached the post season playoffs for the first time in franchise history.

On this day in Sports History, October 23, 1993 Joe Carter, playing for the Toronto Blue Jays hit a ninth inning home run to beat the Philadelphia Phillies to win the 1993 World Series. The Blue Jays had won the World Series the year before, defeating the Atlanta Braves. The Blue Jays are the only team outside of the United States to win the Word Series. (not bad eh?)

On this day in Sports History, September 14, the Toronto Blue jays set a major league record by hitting 10 home-runs in a nine inning game and defeating the Baltimore Orioles 18-3.

On this day in Sports History, October 14, 2003, the Chicago Cubs were leading the Florida Marlins 3-0 in the eighth inning in the sixth game of the National League Championship Series, Marlins batter Luis Castillo hit a foul ball near the stands, when Cubs outfielder, Moises Alou reached up to make the out Cubs fan Steve Bartman reached out over Alou and distracting him from making the out. After the Marlins were spared the out, the Florida Marlins rallied and scored eight runs winning the game and tying the series. Bartman was escorted off the field for his own protection as angry Cub fans yelled angry insults and threw debris at him. The sad part of the Cubs story is that they lost the following night 9-6 in the final game of the series.

In 1963, Mickey Mantle signed $100.000 contract with the New York Yankees, at the time it was the largest contract ever signed in Major League Baseball

On this day in Sports History august 16,1 948; Babe Ruth died of throat cancer,The Sultan of Swat as he was known Hit 714 home runs in his career. He held the record until 1974 when Hank Aaron broke the record

On this day in Sports History April 18, 1923 In the first game played at Yankee Stadium Babe Ruth Homered and the Yankees went on to beat the Boston Red Sox, who had traded Ruth to the New York Yankees,-- 4-1Yankee Stadium became known as The House that Ruth built.

On this day in Sports History, September 24, 1934 Babe Ruth, AKA The Bambino, Made his final appearance as a regular player for the New York Yankee against the Boston Red Sox, The Red Sox won The game 5-0

ON this day in Sports History, August 13, 2007 Phil Rizzuto passed away, Rizzuto was 89. After baseball Rizzuto became the Yankee broadcaste rand for years his catch phrase, "Holy Cow" was well known through-out baseball, another phrase he would shout out was; "What a Huckleberry".

On this day in Sports History June 5, 1989 the Toronto Blue Jays played their first game in the Sky Dome now Rogers Center, they lost the game 5-3 to the Milwaukee Braves. Toronto's first baseman Fred Mcgriff, hit the first home run in the new stadium.

On this day in Sports History May 27, 1968 Montreal Canada was awarded a major league Baseball franchise. The Montreal Expos played in the National league until the 2005 season when they moved the franchise to Washington.

On this day in Sports History, June 12, 1939, The National Baseball Hall of Fame was dedicated in Cooperstown New York

On this day in Sports History, June 11, 1967 The New York Mets and the Chicago Cubs tied a Homerun record by hitting 11 homeruns in a single game. The Mets hit 4 and the Cubs hit 7. In 1950 the New York Yankees hit 6 homers and the Detroit Tigers hit 5

On this day in Sports History, June 11, 1985, Von Hayes Hit 2 home runs in the first inning. The Philadelphia Phillies scored 9 runs in the first inning, and went on to beat the New York Mets 26-7 Von Hayes was the firs player in Baseball history to hit 2 homers in the first inning,

On this day in Sports History June 11, 1990, Nolan Ryan pitched his 6th No Hitter of hi career, He was the oldest player to pitch a no hitter; he was 43 at the time The Texas Rangers beat the Oakland A's 5-0. Nolan was the first Pitcher to throw a No Hitter for 3 different teams.

On this day in Sports History June 11, 1997, Roger Clemens lost on opening day for the first time after 11 strait wins to start the season. The Seattle Mariners beat the Toronto Blue Jays 5-1

On this day in Sports History June 19, 2010, Roberto Alomar, and Paul Quantrill were inducted into the Canadian Baseball Hall of Fame. Alomar was instrumental in the Toronto Blue Jays winning the World Series two years in a row. The Blue Jays won the Series in 1992 and 1993.

On this day in Sports History, September 25, 1920 eight players involved in the "Black Sox Scandal" were exposed and their names made public. The Chicago White Sox players were bribed to deliberately lose the World Series They were banned for life from Major League Baseball

On this day in Sports History September 27,2018,German Marquez, Pitching for the Colosado Rockies, tied a modern major league record by striking out the first eight batters to start a game against Philadelphia.. Two other players have accomplished the modern-day record, they are; New York Mets,righty Jacob deGrom, on Sept. 15, 2014, and,Houston leftyJim Deshaies on September 23, 1986. The record is held by Mickey Welch who struck ut the first nine batters to start a game on August 28, 1884

On this day in Sports History Saturday October 20, 2018 the los angeles Dodgers beat the Milwaukkee Brewers 5-1 in the seventh game of the National league Championship game. On October 28.2018, In the World series the Dodgers Lost 5-1 in the 5th game to the Boston Red Sox.

● ● ● ● ● ● ● ● ● ● ● ● ● ● ● ● ● ● ●

CHAPTER 2

A FEW LEGENDS IN BASEBALL

On this day in Sports History, February 6, 1895 George Herman Ruth Jr. AKA Babe Ruth was born in Baltimore Maryland

On this day in Sports History August 16.1948, Babe Ruth died In Manhattan, New York.

Highlights of Babe Ruth's career

Ruth played 22 seasons in the major leagues from 1914-1935 He Played for the Boston Red Sox,1914—1919,—New York Yankees,1920—1934,—Boston Braves 1935

Babe Ruth's Major league debut was July 11, 1914 with the Boston Red Sox as a pitcher and his last appearance was on May 30th 1935 with the Boston Braves

As a Pitcher his won loss record was 94 wins —46 losses.

His Earned Run Average was 2.28

Babe Ruth was the Earned Run Leader in 1916 playing for The Boston Red Sox

Babe Ruth played 15 years with the New York Yankees.

In the 15 years with the Yankees the team won World Series—7 times 1915—1916—1918—1923—1927—1928— 1932.

Babe Ruth hit 714 home runs while playing for the Yankees.

The Sultan of Swat was the American League home run Champion—12 times—1918—1919 1920— 1921—1923—1924—1926— 1927—1928— 1929 —1930—1931

The Babe was the American League Batting Champion—1924.

Babe Ruth was the R.B.I, leader —6 Ti mes—1919—1920—1921—1923—1926—1928

He was on the All Star team— 2 times. 1933—1934

Ruth was American League M .V.P.in 1923—

Ruth —was an All Star—2 times — 1933—1934—

Babe Ruth Had 2,213 career Runs Batted IN-

Ruth ended up with a 342 batting average

Ruth had 2873 hits in his career

Babe Ruth Had the Home run record of 714 Homers until hank Aaron broke it in !974.

The New York Yankees Retired Babe Ruth's Jersey number 3

Ruth was selected to The Major League All Century Team

Babe Ruth was also selected to the Major League All Time Team

Babe Ruth The Bambino as he was also known was inducted into the Boston Red Sox Hall of Fame (Do You Remember The Curse of The Bambino)

George Herman Babe Ruth Jr. was inducted into the Baseball Hall of Fame in 1936

On this day in Sports History October 29 1931 Mickey Charles Mantle was born In Spavinaw Oklahoma

Mickey Mantle died on August 13, 1995 He was 63 when he passed away in Dallas Texas

Mickey Mantle was considered as one of the greatest center fielders of all time.

Highlights of Mickey Mantle's career

Mantles first appearance for the New York Yankees was on April, 17, 1951, and his last game was on September 28, 1968 for the New York Yankees, As a matter of fact he spent his entire major league career with the Yankees..

Mantle Won The Triple Crown—1 time—1956 .

Mantle was a switch hitter; he had lifetime batting average of 298—

He ended up with536 home runs

Mickey Mantle had 1,509 runs batted in—

He ended his career with 2,415 Hits—

Mantle played in the All Star game—16 times—1952 1953—1954—1955—1956—1957—1958—1959—1960 1961—1962—1963—1964—1965—1967—1968-

Mantle and the Yankees won the World Series—7 times 1951—1952 1953—1956—1958—1961—1962—

Mickey Mantle was the American League MVP — 3 times—1956-1957—1962—

He was a Golden Glove Center Fielder—1 time—1962—

Mantle was the American League batting champion—1 time—1956—

Mickey Mantle was the American League Home Run Champion—1955—1956—1958—1960

Mantle was elected to the Major league Baseball All Century Team in 1999. (And how is that for a major league Baseball career?).

Mickey Charles Mantle was inducted into the National Baseball Hall of Fame In 1974

On this day in Sports History, November 24, 1914 Joe DiMaggio was born in Martinez, California

On this day in Sports History, March 8, 1999, Jolting Joe DiMaggio died at the age of 84 in Hollywood, Florida

DiMaggio is another player that played his entire career with the New York Yankees. He played 13 seasons with the Yankees

Joe DiMaggio made his first appearance for the New York Yankees on May, 3, 1936 and made his final appearance on September 30, 1951 for the New York Yankees.

Highlights of Joe DiMaggio's career

Joe DiMaggio's life time Batting Average was 325—

DiMaggio had 1,537 runs batted in—

He had a total of 2,214 hits in his career

DiMaggio hit 361 home runs For the Yankees

He was a Three Time American League MVP—3 times—1939—1941—1947

He was on the All Star team in each of his 13 years as a Yankee.

As a Yankee he and the team won American League Pennant—10 times

DiMaggio and the Yankees won The World Series—9 times;—1936—1937—1938—1939—1941—1947—1949—1950—1951 — (Holy ——!)

He was American League Batting Champion—2 times—1939—1940—

He was the American League Home Run Leader—2 times—1937—1948

Joe DiMaggio holds the record that many, many experts in the game of baseball believe will never be broken; His 56 game hitting streak. Joe DiMaggio hit safely in 56 games in a row games. His hitting streak started on May 15, and ended July 16, 1941

DiMaggio also had a hitting streak of 61 in the Pacific Coast League in California

Joe DiMaggio was married twice, his first wife was Dorothy Arnold, his second wife was the famous Movie Star Marilyn Monroe. (WHAT A LUCKY GUY). The marriage did not last long, but he was loyal to her for the rest of her life

Joe DiMaggio's Jersey number 5 was retired by the New York Yankees

He was selected to the Major League All Century Team.

Joe Paul DiMaggio was inducted into the Baseball Hall of Fame in 1955

On this Day un Sports History June 19, 1903 Louis Gehrig was born in Yorkville, Manhattan New York.

On this day in Sports History Lou Gehrig died on June 2, 1941 Lou Gehrig died. Gehrig was only 37 when he passed away in Riverdale, Bronx, New York City

Highlight of Lou Gehrig's career

Gehrig started his career on June 15, 1923 for the New York Yankees. Gehrig played all his 17 years in the Major Leagues with the Yankees; from 1923—1939

His first major league appearance was on June 15, 1915 and his Last appearance was on April 30, 1939

Lou Gehrig had a lifetime batting average of. 340

Gehrig batted left and threw left.

Gehrig had 1,995 runs batted in—

He Had 2,721 career hits—

He hit 493 home runs—

Gehrig was an All Star— 7 times—1933—1934—1935—1936—1937—1938—1939.—

Gehrig was on World Series Championships Teams— 6 times—1927—1928—1932—1936—1937—1938.

Lou Gehrig was the American League Most Valuable Player 2 Times—1927—and 1936

He was the Triple Crown winner; (Home runs—Runs Batted In—and Batting Average)—1 time—1934-

Lou Gehrig was the American League Batting Champion—1 time 1934—

Gehrig was the American league Home Run Leader— 3 times—1931—1934—1936

He was RBI Leader— 5 times—191927—1928—1930—1931—and1934

On June 3, 1932 Gehrig hit 4 home runs in one game

He was the New York Yankees Captain —1935—1936—1937—1938—1939—

Gehrig was selected to the All-Time Team—

Major League Baseball All Century Team—

In 1969 thirty years after he retired the Baseball Writers Association voted Lou Gehrig the greatest first baseman of all time.

Lou Gehrig was the first player in the Major leagues to have his uniform number (4) Retired,

Henry Louis Gehrig was inducted into National Baseball Hall of Fame in 1939

On this day in Sports History, August 30, 1918, Theodore Samuel Williams was born in San Diego California

Ted Williams Passed away on July 5, 2002 at the age of 93 in Inverness Florida

Ted Williams aka Teddy Ballgame—The Kid—The Thumper—The Splendid Splinter—and The Greatest Hitter Who Ever Lived.

Ted Williams was a true and loyal American hero that served his country in world war two for 3 years from 1943 to 1947 and he also served in the Korean War, as a Marine combat aviator in 1952 and 1953.

Ted Williams made his debut as the left fielder on April, 20th 1939 for the Boston Red Sox, and he played his last game for the Red Sox on September 28 1960. Williams played his entire baseball Career with the Red Sox

Highlights of Ted Williams Major League Career

Ted Williams Had a Life time Batting average of—344

Ted Williams hit 521 Home Runs—

Williams had 1839 Runs batted in—

Williams had 2654 Hits—

His on base percentage was—.482 (This was amazing)

He was the manager for the Texas Rangers and the Washington Senators—1969—1972—

Ted Williams was selected to the All Star Game— 17 times and would have been 19 times had he not been serving his country for 3 years. 1940—1941—1942—1946—1947—1948—1949—1950—1951—1953—1954—1955—1956—1957—1958—1959—1960

American League Most Valuable Player—2 Times—1946—1949—

Williams won the Triple Crown 2 times—1942—1947— (The leader for the season in Home Runs—Runs Batted, in—and Batting Average)

Ted Williams was the American League Batting Champion—6 times—1941—1942—1947—1948—1857—1958—

He was the American League RBI Leader— 4 times—1939—1942—1947—1949

Ted Williams was the American League Home Run leader— 4 times—1941—1942—1947—1949—

He has the Major League Record for an on- base percentage of .482 for his career.

The Boston Red Sox retired his Number 9 Jersey

The Boston Red Sox Inducted Williams into the Red Sox Hall of Fame

Williams was selected to the Major League Baseball All Time Team—

He was selected to the Major League All Century Team

Theodore Samuel Williams was inducted into the Major League Baseball Hall of Fame in; !966—He Received 93.4% of the votes on the First Ballot

On this day in Sports History, May 6, 1931 Willie Howard Mays Jr. was born in Westfield Alabama.

Willie Mays, AKA, The Say Hey Kid was one of the most exciting players to ever play in the Major leagues. The name of the game is Hit—Run—and catch—and he did the combination better than anybody.

Highlights of Willie Mays Major Leagues career

Rookie of the Year—1951

Mays debut was May25, 1951 for the New York Giants hast Major league appearance was September 9, 1973 for the New York Mets

Mays batting average was302—

Willie Mays had 3,283 Hits—

He had 1903 Runs Batted in —

Willie Mays had 338 Stolen Bases—

Mays hit 660 home runs he was third on the list at the time of his retirement.

He played for New York Giants—1951-1952—

San Francisco Giants— 1954—1972—(19 years)

He ended his career with the New York Mets in 1973

Mays was an All Star 19 times— 1954—1973—

The San Francisco Giants won the World Series—1 time—1954

Mays was The National League Most Valuable Player— 2 times —1954— and 1965

Gold Glove Award 12 times—1957—1958—1959—1960—1961—1962— 1963—1964—1965—1966—1967—1968

Mays won the Roberto Clemente Award—1971

Mays was The National League Batting Champion—1time 1954—

He was The National League Home Run Leader 4 times —1955—1962—1964— 1965

Willie Mays was The Nation league Stolen Base Leader 4 times —1956—1957—1958—1959—

Mays hit 4 home runs in one game on April 30, 1961

San Francisco Giants retired uniform number 24.

Mays was elected to the Major League All Time Team—

Willie Howard Mays Jr. was inducted into the National Baseball Hall of Fame in 1979. He received 94.7 % on the first ballot.

On this day in Sports History December 30, 1935 Sanford Braun was born in Brooklyn New York.

He became one of the greatest pitchers in baseball history, he was better known as Sandy Koufax

Koufax pitched for 12 years in the Majors, from 1955—1966.

Since I was an avid San Francisco Giants fan, Koufax was not one of my favorite players. If you knew about the Giants and Dodgers rivalry in the 50s and 60s you would understand why. I don't know of 2 teams that disliked each other more.

Highlights of Sandy Koufax's Major League Career

Koufax was a left handed pitcher and batted right handed.

Koufax made his first appearance for the Brooklyn Dodgers on June 24, 1955, and his final appearance on October2, 1966 for the Los Angeles Dodgers.

On this day in sports history September 9, 1965 at 9:46 In Los Angeles California Sandy Koufax struck out Harvey Kuenn, to finish with what is known as a perfect game against the Chicago Cubs. That is no runs and no hits. He faced the minimum of 27 batters. That means 27 up and 27 down. The Dodgers won the game 1-0 As it turned out he needed the no, no because the opposing Pitcher, Bob Hendley had pitched a great game himself, He had a 1 hit game to lose one of the greatest Pitching duels in Baseball History.

Koufax had pitched 3 other no hitters earlier in his career, but this one was extra special. Koufax's 4 no hitters stood as a record until Nolan Ryan broke the record with his 5th No No, in 1981: Nolan Ryan holds the current record today with 7 No Hitters.

Koufax won loss record stands at 165 wins —87 losses.—

His earned Run Average was 2.76—

Koufax struck out 2,396 Batters—

He was an All Star—6 times— 1961—1962-1963—1964—1965—1966

He was on the Dodger team that w on the World Series Championship — 4 times—1955—1959—1963—1965

He won the World Series Most Valuable Player Award—2 times1963—1965

He was national League Most Valuable Player 1 time—1963—

He won The Cy Young award— 3 times—1963—1965—1966—

Sandy Koufax was the Major League wins leader—3 times—1963—1965—1966—

National League ERA leader— 2 times—1962—1966

Major League Strike Out Leader 4 times—1961—1963—1965—1966

The Dodgers retired number 32

He is on The Major League All-Century Team.

He is on the Major League Baseball All Time Team.

Sandy Koufax was inducted into the National Baseball Hall Of Fame in 1972

⊙ᚙᚙ⊙

● ● ● ● ● ● ● ● ● ● ● ● ● ● ● ● ● ●

CHAPTER 3

ON THIS DAY IN SPORTS
HISTORY FOOTBALL

On this day in Sports History February 3, 2019 Tom brady played in his 40th play-off game at the age of 40. He was 40 on august the 3rd..He is the oldest player to ever win a Super Bowl at the age of

On this day in Sports History January, 20, 2019 the Los Angeles Rams defeated the New Orleans Saints 26 to 23 to win the NFC Championship in the NFL. Quarterback Jared Goff passed foe 297 yards, he completed 25 passes out of 40 Attempts.Goff had 1 touchdown pass and he threw 1 interception Brandin Cooks was the leading reciever for the Rams with 7 receptions for 107 yards. C.J. Anderson was the leading rusher for the Rams with 16 carries for 44 yards.

Drew Brees of the New Orleans Saints passed for 249 yards, he had 2 touchdown passes and 1 interception.He atteempted 40 passes and completed 26. The leading reciever for the Saints was Alvin Kamara; he had 11 receptions for 96 yards. The leader in rushing for the Saints was Mark Ingram Jr. with 9 Carries for 31 yards.

On this day in Sports History Monday January 28 2019, an article came out in the Ottawa Sun newspaper here in Canada that a Louisiana based eye-care business is offering N.F.L. referees free eye exams before the 2019- 20 season." After having time to consider things we will GLADLY provide no-cost eye exams to all NFL officials prior to next season to prevent the atrocity that occurred tonight (Sunday). We would hate for someone else to feel our pain"said a Louisiana Family Eyecare.This was just one response to a very very contoversial call, close to the end of the NFC championship game between the L.A.. Rams and the New Orleans Saints.

On this day in Sports History,Saturday Febuary 2nd Patriick Mahomes was selected By the Associated Press the NFL's Mostaluable Player and offensive player of the year.

Mahomes threw for 50 touchdowns and a total of 5,097 yds. Patrich Maomes had a quarterback rating of113.8, only Drew Brees had a little higher rating.

On this Day in Sports History,January 20,2019 the New England Patriots defeated the Kansas City Chiefs by the score of 37 t0 31 to win the AFC division of the NFL..The Patriots were led by the great Tom Brady at quarterback Brady passed for 348 yards, he completed 30 of 46 attempts, he had 2 touchdown passes and I interception.

The leading reciever for the Patriots was Gronkowski, who had 6 receptions for 79 yards; the leader in rushing for the Patriots was Sony Michel with 29 carries for 113 yards

The quarterback for K.C. was -Mahomes who is also a great quarterback, He is young,but as good as any quarterback in the NFL and better than Most.Mahomes passed for 295 yards with 3 touchdown passes and no interceptions, he completed 16 of 31 attempts. Kelce had 3 receptions for 23 yards and 1 T.D.

On this day in Sports History The New England patriots won Super Bowl XIII (53) by deafeating the Los Angeles Rams by the Score of 13 to 3.

Quarterback Tom Brady Passed for 262 yards, He attempted 35 passes and completed 21. He did not have a T.D. and he threw 1 intercepyion.

The leading receiver was Julian Edelman; he had 10 receptions for a total of 141 yards.

The leader in rushing was Sony Michel, he had 18 carries for 94 yards and had the only touchdown of the game.

The quarterback for the L.A. Rams was Jared Goff. Goff attempted 38 passes and he completed 19, for a total of 229 yards, He did not have a T.D and he threw I very crucial Interception.

The leader in receiving for the Rams was Brandin Cooks, he had 8 receptions for 120 yards

The Leading Rusher for the Rams was Todd Gurley, who had 10 carries for 35 yards.

THE FOLLOWING ARE INTERESTING FACTS AND RECORDS BROKEN IN SUPER BOWL 53

1. Tom Brady became the first Quarterback or player to win **6** Superbowl championship rings.
2. Tom Brady at the age of 41 set the record as the oldes Q.B. to win a Super Bowl
3. Bill Belichick joined George Halas The great couch for the Chicago Bears and Curly Lambeau with **6** SUPER Bowl wins as a couch
4. Bill Belichick at the age of 66 became the oldest head coach to win the Super Bowl
5. with the win the Patrios have won 37 post season games, which passed the Pittsburg Steeler that have 36 post season wins.
6. As a player coach combination Belichick and Brady have a record of six wins and 3 losses in the Super Bowl More than twice as many as any other Q.B. Coach combination.
7. The Coach for the L. A. Rams Sean McVay was the youngest coach to ever coach in the Super Bowl.

8. Tom Brady set the record for the most career passes in Super-Bowl history with 392 attepts and 256 completions.
9. The 65 yard punt was the longest Punt in Super Bowl History
10. One touchdown by both teams is now the record for the fewest Touchdowns in the Super Bowl.
11. The Patriots set the record for the fewest points scored by the wiining team in the Super Bowl
12. The two teams set the record for the fewest points scored by both teams; New England Patriots13 and the Los Angeles Rams 3.

Juian Edelman was selected as the Most Valuable Player in Super Bowl 53. Edelman Had a fantastic day avoiding the pass defence, there was just now way The Rams defence could cover Julian Ededlman one on one on this particular day!

The following is a list of all 53 MVP"S in the Super

Bowl

1967 # 1—Bart Starr—QB—Green Bay Packers.
1968 #2-- Bart Starr— QB—Green BayPackers.
1969 # 3-- Joe Namath—QB—New York Jets
1970 # 4-- Len Dawson—QB —Kansas City Chiefs
1971 # 5 Chuck Howley—Linebacker—Dallas Cowboys
1972 # 6-- Roger Staubach—Q.B.—Dallas Cowboys
1973 # 7-- Jake Scott –Safety—Miami Dolphins
1974 # 8—Larry Csonka-- Running Back—Miami Dolphins
1975 #9—Franco Harris—Running Back-Pittsburg Steelers
1976 #10—Lynn Swan—wide reciever—Pittsburg Steelers
1977 #11—Fred Biletnikoff wide reciever—Oaland Raiders
1978 # 12—Harvey Martin—D.E &.Randy White D.T.—Dallas Cowboys
1979 # 13--Terry Bradshaw—Q.B.—Pittsburg Steelers
1980 # 14—Terry Bradshaw—Q.B.—Pittsburg Steelers
1981 # 15—Jim Plunkett —Q.B.—Oakland. Raiders
1982 # 16— Joe Montana—Q.B. San Francisco —49ers
1983 # 17 —John Riggins —Running Back –Washington Redskins

1984 # 18—Marcus Allen –Running Back-- L.A Raiders
1985 # 19—Joe Montana—Q.B. San Francisco—49ers
1986 # 20—Richard Dent—D.E.--Chicago Bears
1987 # 21—Phil Simms—Q. B.—New York Giants
1988 # 22--Doug Williams—Q.B.— Wasington Redskins
1989 # 23—Jerry Rice—W.R. San Francisco 49ers
1990 # 24—Joe Montana—Q.B.—San Francisco 49ers
1991 # 25—Ottis Anderson—Running Back—Washington Redskins
1992 # 26—Mark Rypien—Q.B –Washington Redskins
1993 # 27—Troy Aikman —Q.B-- Dallas Cowboys
1994 # 28—Emmitt Smith—Running Back—Dallas Cowboys
1995 # 29—Steve Young-- Q.B.—San Francisco 49ers
1996# 30—Larry Brown—Cornerback—Dallas Cowboys
1997 # 31—Desmond Howard—Kick & Punt returns Green Bay Packers
1998 # 32—Terrell Davis—Running Back—Denver Broncos
1999 # 33—John Elway—Q. B.—Denver Broncos
2000 # 34—Kurt Warner—Q. B.—St. Louis Rams
2001 # 35—Ray Lewis—Linebacker —Baltimore Ravens
2002 # 36—Tom Brady-- Q. B. -- New England Patriots
2003 # 37— Dexter Jackson—Safety-- Tampa Bay Buccaneers
2004 # 38—Tom Brady—Q.B.—New England Patriots
2005 # 39—Deion Branch—Wide receiver—New England Patriots
2006 # 40—Hines Ward—Wide Receiver— Pittsburg Steelers
2007 # 41—peyton Manning—Q.B.— Indianapolis Colts
2008 # 42—Eli Manning —Q.B.—New York Giants
2009 # 43—Santonio Holmes—Wide Receiver—Pittsburg Steelers
2010 # 44—Drew Brees—Q. B.—New Orleans Saints
2011 # 45—Aaron Rogers—Q.B.— Green Bay Packers
2012# 46—Eli Manning—Q.B. —New York Giants
2013 # 47— Joe Flacco—Q.B.—Baltimore Ravens
1014 # 48—Malcolm Smith—Line-Backer—Seattle Seahawks
2015 # 49—Tom Brady—Q.B.—New England Patriots
2016 # 50—Von Miller—Defensive End—Denver Broncos
2017 # 51—Tom Brady—B.Q. —New England Patriots
2018 #52—Nick Foles—Q.B.— Philladelphia Eagles
2019 # 53—Julian Edelman—Wide receiver—New England Patriots

On this day in Sports History,Tuesday, October 9, 2018 Alex Spanos died in Stockton California. Just a short 2 months and 2 day earlier on August 7th he lost his lovely wife Faye. Alex was 95 and Faye was 92. Stockton is also my home town where I went through school from the first grade, graduated from high school and 2 years of college, so I got to know Alex and his son Dino very well.Alex was a very good golfer and I am a life member of the PGA, so we had some good golf matches in Amateur club tournaments. I do not recall who won the most matches, but it was close. Alex loved golf so much he built a beutiful golf course in Stckton,named after him; Spanos Park.He also loved Stockton nd donated millions of dollars to his home town and to the University of the Pacific. (UOP) Alex Spnos 's father was was a Greek Immigrant, His son went on to amass a fortune in construction and real estate, and then went on to buy the San Diego Chargers Of the NFL in 1984.

On this day in Sports History, December 4, 2018 the Washington Redskins were considering bringing in Collin Kaepernick for a workout to join the Redskins at Quarterback, because of the season ending injury to quarterback Colt Mckoy,but.Coach Jay Gruden decided against the move. Kaepernick has not played in the NFL since the 2016 Season, because he refused to stand during the playing of the National Anthem before the start of football games in the NFL to call attention to police brutality against African Americans, and racial inequities in America. It is not my place to judge what another person does with his or her life, I believe that we should all live our lives the way we want as long as it is not against the law or against the law of our church.

Now ask yourself: Did Kaepernick's protest do as much harm to our country as our current polititions are doing to our country today???/

On this day in Sports History, December 15,1933 the inaugural NFL Championship Football game was played, The Cicago Bears Beat the New York Giants by the score of 23–21 The Game was held at Wrigly Field In Chicago

On this day in sports history, December 28 1958, Johnny Unitas of the Baltimore Colts Playing against the New York Giants for the NFL Championship, in the game that has been described as the greatest football game that has ever been played. Unitas led the Colts to victory and the Championship. Johnny Unitas held the record for fifty two years for the most consecutive games with a touchdown pass.

On this day in Sports History, December 16th 1973, O J Simpson became the first player in the National Football League to rush for more than 2,000 yards in a single season. O J. is the only player to do this in a 14 game schedule. O.J was a 4 time rushing yards leader Unless his record has been broken since he retired. He holds the Single Season Yards Per Game Record. As a sports fan It hurts to see such a great athlete have the very serious problems O J Simpson has endured.

In 1995 in one of the most sensational trials in American history O. J Simpson was found not guilty of Murder in the deaths of his ex wife Nicole Brown and Ronald Coleman

On this day in Sports History December 6, 2008 O.J. Simpson was sentenced to 33 years in prison, He was released on parole after serving 9 years. Simpson was found guilty of kidnapping and robbing two memorabilia dealers in Las Vegas in 2007

On this day in Sports History, November 12, 1995 Dan Marino broke Fran Tarkenton's record to become the NFL's All Time Passing Yards Leader. Marino led the Miami Dolphins to the NFL Playoffs 10 times in his 17 year career After retirement in he worked foe CBS as a football analyst. In 2014 he was the special adviser for the Dolphins The Dan Marino Foundation, a charitable organization has raised more than 53 million dollars to help individuals with Autism and other developmental disabilities.

On this day in Sports History, September 7th 1980 the Green Bay Packers and the Chicago Bears were tied at 6 to 6 in overtime at Lambeau Field. Chester Marcol of the Green Bay was set to kick a 35 yard field to win the game when Alan Page of the Bears blocked the field goal attempt,

The ball ended up in the hands of Marcol who broke free around the left end and outran the Bears players that were confused and surprised by what just happened. The touchdown gave the packers a 12 to 6 win.

On this day in Sports History January 1st, 1929 Georgia Tech was playing in the Rose Bowl against the California Golden Bears. There was a capacity crowd of 70,000 watching the game. In the 2nd quarter one of the most unusual plays in football history occurred in this game. Roy Riegels of the Bears playing the center position was the captain elect for the Bears, scooped up a Georgia Tech fumble, he started towards the tech end zone, but as he was trying to elude the tech players he got confused and started back towards the California End zone. Benny Lom the halfback for the Bears chased Reagles and finally caught him on the 3 yard line, the tech playes hit him and he ended up on the one yard line. The Bears got in the punt formation, the ball was snapped Maree the defensive tackle for Georgia Tech blocked the punt and it rolled out of the end zone, the referees ruled that the ball was touched by the quarterback and a safety would be scored against the California Bears. Tech won the game 8—7 because of the Safety

On this day in Sports History May 1, 1909 The Grey cup was donated for the Canadian football championship named in honor of Governor General Earl Grey. The condition of the cup was that it was to remain always under purely amateur conditions. The Grey Cup is now a contest to determine the champion of the Canadian Football League..

On this day in Sports History, September 1, 1990, The Toronto Argonauts and the British Columbia Lions set a new CFL record by combining for 111 points in a 68-43 win by Toronto at the (Sky Dome, now named Rogers Center)—they also set a record of 50 points in the second quarter, 27 points by Toronto and 23 by the Lions.

On this day in Sports History, February I, 2015, At Glendale Arizona The New England Patriots were playing against the defending Super Bowl champions Seattle Seahawks in Super Bowl XLIX. One of the key plays in the game New England Patriots Malcolm Butler intercepts a pass intended for Seattle Seahawks wide receiver Ricardo Lockette in the Second Half of the game. The Patriots went on to win the game 28-24Tom Brady completed 37 of 50 Passes and was named MVP of the game. Super Bowl XLIX became the most watched program in NBC network history

On this day in Sports History, December 23 1962 the Dallas Texans defeated the AFL Champions Houston Oilers 20-17 in double overtime to win their third AFL Title. The next year the Texans relocated to Kansas City, and became what we know today as the Kansas City Chiefs..

In the 1950 season Marion Motley of the Cleveland Browns set a single game record, He had 10 attempts for an amazing 17.1 yards per carry

On this day in Sports History, February 1, 2009 The Pittsburg Steelers Became the first team in the NF history to win 6 Super Bowls with A win over the Arizona Cardinals 27-23

On this ay in Sports HistoryJanuary 12, 1969 Joe Namath quarterback for the new Yort Jets upset the Baltimore Colts in SuperBowl 3 to a 16-7 win. This was and still is one of the biggest upsets in Sports History. The Colts had lost only one game that season. The quarterback for the Colts was the Great Johnny Unitas.

On this day in Sports History Monday January, 7, 2019 the Clemson Tiger won the College National Championship by deafeating the Alabama Crimson Tide by the score of 44-16. Both teams were 14-0 for the season. Clemson was coached by Dabo Swinney, and Alabama was coached by Nick Saban. Saban is a former NFL coach. Clemson is in the ACC conference and Alabama Plays in the SEC.

● ● ● ● ● ● ● ● ● ● ● ● ● ● ● ● ● ●

CHAPTER 4

A FEW LEGENDS IN FOOTBALL

Vincent Thomas Lombardi was born in Brooklyn New York on June 11, 1913

On this day in Sports History September 3, 197o, Vince Lombardi died

It is well established that Vince Lombardi is considered by many as the greatest coach in the history of the NFL and many consider him as the greatest coach in any sport.

Lombardi's winning percentage in the NFL is 719—His win loss record was 96 Wins—34 Losses—6 Ties

His playoff record was 9—1 (90%)

He had an overall record of—105—35—6

Lombardi coached The Green Bay Packers from—1959—1967— He coached The Washington Redskins in 1969—

Vince Lombardi never had a Losing Season as a Head Coach. .

At Green Bay He Led the Packers to 3straight championships.

Lombardi's team, (The Packers) won the NFL Championship 5 times--

He won the first two Super Bowls—

The Super Bowl Trophy Is named after Vince Lombardi

He was the General Manager of the Green Bay Packers—1968

Twice he was named coach of the year —2 Times—1959—and 1961—

Lombardi's Team won the first Super Bowls —1—and 2—

His team won 6 NFL
championships—1956—1961—1962—1965—1966—1967—

He is in the Green Bay Hall of Fame—

Lombardi is in the Washington Ring of Fame.

Not only was Vince Lombardi great coach but he was also a great human being and a great role model for future coaches and players

The following are a few Quotes by the great coach Vince Lombardi—1913—1970

There is no room for second place. There is only one place in my game and that is first place. I have finished second twice in my time at Green Bay and I never want to finish second again.

Winning isn't everything, it's the only thing.

Winning is a habit. Unfortunately so is losing.

The achievements of an organization are the results of the combined effort of each individual

People who work together will win, whether it be against a complex football defense, or the problems in modern society

Individual commitment to a group effort—that is what makes a team work, a company work, a society work, civilization work

It is easy to have faith in yourself and have discipline when you are a winner, when you're number one, What you got to have is faith and discipline when you are not a winner.

It is not whether you get knocked down it's whether you get up

Show me a good loser, and I will show you a loser

Once you learn to quit, it becomes a habit.

Winners never quit and quitters never win

Coaches who can outline plays on the blackboard are a dime a dozen. The ones who win get inside their players and motivate.

Confidence is contagious. So is lack of confidence.

If it doesn't matter who wins or loses, the why do they keep score?

Vincent Thomas Lombardi was inducted into The Football hall of Fame in 1971one year after he died.

⚭

On this day in Sports History,,Joe Clifford Montana Jr. was born June 11, 1956 in New Eagle Pennsylvania

Joe Montana also known as Joe Cool or The Comeback Kid was one was one of the very best Quarterbacks in the history of the N.F.L. Montana was a legend in his own time. I was fortunate to be a Forty 49er fan Since the 1950s, As a matter of fact I was lucky enough that through certain connections I got one of the watches that the Forty 49er players got when they won the Super Bowl two years in a row, the sad thing that a very good friend of mine Bob Sollis also an avid San Francisco Forty 49er fan offered me $ 2,000 for the watch and Like a Dummy it and I sold it to him..

Highlights of Joe Montana's NFL career

Prior to being drafted by San Francisco Montana led Notre Dame to the College National Championship—1977Joe Montana Was drafted by the Forty 49ers in the 3rd, round and was picked 82nd.in the draft.

Montana Played for San Francisco from 1979—1992 and for the Kansas City Chiefs 1993—1994.

With Montana at quarterback the 49ers won the Super bowl—4 times they won Super Bowl—XV1—X1X—XXIII—XXIV Montana was Selected the M V P in three of those Super Bowls—XV1—X1X—XX1V—

He was selected to the Pro Bowl Games—8 times—1981—1983—1994—1985—1987—1989—1990—1993

He was selected to The First Team All- Pro—3 times—1987—1989—1990—

Montana was selected to the second team All-pro 2 times—1981—1984-

Montana was selected as the NFL most valuable player 2 times—1989—and 1990-

Joe Montana was selected NFL offensive player of the year 1 time—1989—

Bert Bell Award—1989—

Sports Illustrated Sportsman of the year—1990—

Montana was A.P. Athlete of the Year 2 times—1989—1990—

Montana was NFL Comeback Player of the Year 1 time—1986—

He was NFL passer rating leader 2 times—1987—1989—

Joe Montana was the Passing touchdown leader 2 times—1982—1987

He was selected to The NFL 1980s All Decade Team

He was selected to the NFL 75th Anniversary All Time Team

San Francisco 49ers retired Number 16

Joseph Clifford Montana Jr. was inducted into the Pro Football Hall of Fame in 2000 on his first year of eligibility

On this day in Sports History May 7, 1933 John Constantine Unitas was born in Pittsburg Pennsylvania

Johnny U. as he was known died on, September 11, 2002 John Constantine Unitas died at the age of 69.

Without a doubt Johnny Unitas became one of the greatest Quarterbacks in NFL history. If you heard his nickname Johnny U. or the golden arm you knew they were talking about Johnny Unitas.

Highlights of Johnny Unitas's NFL career

Unitas was drafted in 1955 by the Pittsburg Steelers in the ninth round and was the 102nd ver—

From 1956—1972 he played for the Baltimore Colts—and ended his career with the San Diego Chargers in 1973

With Johnny U at quarterback, The Baltimore Colts won Super Bowl V

He led the Colts to the NFL Championship 3 times—1958—1959—1968

He was selected to the Pro Bowl Game 10 times—1957—1958—1959 1960—1961—1962— 1963—1964—1966—and 1967.

He was First Team All Pro 5 times—1958—1959—1964—1965—1967

He was second team All Pro 2 times —1957—1963

Johnny Unitas was named AP NFL Most Valuable Player 3 times—1959—1964—1967

Bert Bell Award 3 Times—1959—1964—1967

He was voted NFL Man of the Year—1970

Johnny U. was NFL passing yards leader 4 times—1957—1959—1960—and 1963

John Unitas was the NFL passing touchdown leader 4 times—1957—1958—1959—1960

Johnny U. attempted 5,186 and completed 2,830—

John Unitas ended his great career with 290 touchdowns—

40,239 Yards Passing—

A passing rating of 78.2.

He was elected to the1960s All Decade Team

He was elected to the NFL 75th Anniversary All Time Team.

(How good must you be to be elected to the 1960s All Decade Team and the NFL All Time Team???)

The Indianapolis Colts retired his jersey number 19

THE Louisville Cardinals retired number 16.

John Constantine Unitas was inducted into the National Football Hall Of Fame In 1979

On this day in Sports History; October 13, 1962 Jerry Lee Rice was born.—Rice was born in Starkville Mississippi

Jerry Rice played for 20 years in the NFL

If he is not the greatest player of all time in the NFL, then he is a close second or third (He is not a bad dancer either—Dancing with the stars)

Highlights of Jerry Rice's career in the NFL

Jerry Rice was drafted by the San Francisco 49ers in 1985 in the first round and was picked 16th over- all.

He played for the San Francisco 49ers—From 1985— 2000-

Rice played for The Oakland Raiders from—2001—2004—

He played for the Seattle Seahawks—2004—

He played for the Denver Broncos—2005

Rice was considered by many as the greatest wide receiver in NFL history. Many football experts say number 80 was the greatest NFL player of all time

Jerry Rice was the MVP in Super Bowl XX111

Jerry Rice was on 3 Super Bowl Championship teams 3 times—XX111—XX1V—XX1X

He was selected to the Pro Bowl 13 times—1986—1987—1988— 1989—1990—1991—1992—1993—1994—1995—1996—1998—2002—

Jerry Rice was selected to The First team All Pro 10 times—1986— 1987—1988—1989—1990—1992—1993—1994—1995—1996

He was selected to the 2nd team All Pro 2 times—1991—2002

PFWA NFL Most Valuable Player 1 time—1987

Bert Bell Award—1987

Jerry Rice was Offensive Player of the year 2 times—1987—1990

Rice was the NFL Receiving Yards Leader 6 times—1986—1989—1990—1993—1994—1995—

He was the NFL reception leader 2 times—1990—1996—

Jerry Rice was the NFL receiving touchdown leader6 ti mes—1986—1987—1989—1990—1991—1993

Rice was selected to the NFL 75th Anniversary All Time Team—

Jerry Rice was selected to the 1980s All Decade Team—

He was also selected to the 1990s All Decade team

Jerry Rice was First Team 1AA All American— 1983—1984

Jerry Rice has the NFL Record for Receptions—1,549

Jerry Rice holds the record for Receiving Yards—22,895

Rice holds the NFL record for receiving Touchdowns—197 He has the record for all purpose yards—23,546

The San Francisco 49ers Retired Number 80

Jerry Rice was inducted into the College Football Hall Of Fame on august 12, 2006

Jerry Lee Rice was inducted into the Pro Football Hall of Fame in 2010.

On this day in Sports History; February 17, 1936, James Nathaniel Brown was born In St. Simmons Georgia.

Jim Brown is considered as the greatest **fullback** in history and he is among the greatest football players of all time. In 2002 The Sporting News named Jim Brown as the greatest football player ever.

Highlights of Jim Brown's career in the NFL

Brown was selected in the draft in 1957 in the first round and was the 6th player picked by the Cleveland Browns, where he played from 1957-1965. He played college football at Syracuse University in New York where he was a unanimous All American. In 1995 he was inducted into the College Football Hall of Fame.

As a professional he carried the ball 2,359 for a total of 12,312 rushing yards

He led the Browns to the NFL championship —1964

Jim Brown was selected to The Pro Bowl each year he was in the league—9 times — 1957—1958— 1959—1960—1961—1962—1963—1964—1965—

He was NFL Rookie of the year—1957

The Bert Bell Award—1963

First team All Pro 8 times—1957—1958—1959—1960—1961—1963— 1964—1965—(what the hell happened in 62—????)

Jim Brown was The AP NFL Most valuable Player 3 times—1957—1958—1965

Brown was the Rushing Leader 8 times—1957—1958—1959—1960— 1961—1963—1964—1965—(there's that 62 again).

Jim Brown's Yards Per Carry was—5.2 Yards

He was the NFL Rushing touchdown leader 5 times—1957—1958 —1959—1963—1965—

Jim Brown had a Total of —106 Touchdowns

He had —262—Receptions

Brown had—2,499—Receiving Yards

Jim Brown had 20 Receiving –touchdowns—

Brown was selected to The NFL All Decade Team—

He was selected to The NFL 75th Anniversary All Time Team

Cleveland Browns Retired Browns jersey; Number 32 —

Syracuse University Retired Number 44

Jim Brown was inducted into the College Football Hall of Fame Inducted In 1995 James Nathaniel Brown was inducted into the Pro Football Hall of Fame in 1971

On this day in Sports History July 25, 1954 Walter Jerry Payton was born in Columbus Mississippi

On this day in Sports History, November 1, 1999 Walter Payton died at the age of 45

Highlights of Walter Payton's NFL career

Payton was drafted by the Chicago Bears in 1975 in the first round and was the 4th man picked over-all.

He played for the Bears from 1975—1987

He led the Bears to a Super Bowl win Super Bowl champions XX

Payton was selected to the Pro Bowls Games 9 times—1976—1977—1978—1979—1980—1983—1984—1985—1986—

He was selected to the First Team ALL Pro7 times—1976—1977—1978—1979—1980—1985—1985—

Payton was also selected to the second team All Pro 1 time—1986

Payton was selected by the AP the NFL Most Valuable Player 1 time—1977

He received the Bert Bell Award —1985

NFC Offensive Player of the Year 2 times—1977—1985

NFL Offensive Player of the Year—1977

NFL Man of the Year—1977

NFL Rushing Yards Leader—1977

NFL Rushing Touchdown Leader—1977

Walter Payton was selected to the 1970s All Decade Team—

He was selected to The NFL 75th Anniversary All Time Team.

Chicago Bears Jersey number 34 was retired

In his career at Chicago Walter Payton Rushed for 16,726—

He averaged 4.4 yards per carry—

He scored 110 Rushing Touchdowns—

He had 492 receptions for 4,538 yards—

He scored15 receiving Touchdowns—

He was inducted into the College Football Hall of Fame.

Walter Payton was a nice man

Walter Jerry Payton was inducted into the NFL Pro Football Hall Of Fame in 1993.

On this Day in Sports History, July 16, 1968 Barry Sanders was born in Wichita Kansas

Barry Sanders was drafted By the Detroit Lions in the first round and was the 3rd man picked He played for Detroit from 1989—1998.Barry Sanders retired from football after the 1998 season.

Highlights of Barry Sanders NFL career

Barry Sanders as junior at Oklahoma State had one of the most remarkable seasons in college history. He rushed for 2,850 yards—was a unanimous All American—won the Heisman Trophy and was inducted into The College Football Hall of Fame in 2003

He was elected to the Pro Bowl every year he played—10 times—1989 —1990—1991—1992—1993—1994—1995—1996—1997—1998—

Barry Sanders was First team All-Pro—6 times—1989— 1990—1991—1994—1995—1997—

He was Second team All-Pro —4 times—1992—1993—1996—and 1998—

Barry Sanders was chosen The NFL Most Valuable Player—1997—

NFL Offensive Player of The Year—2 times—1994—199

The Bert Bell Award—2 times1991—1997—

NFL Rushing Yards Leader—4 times—1990—1994—1996—1997

NFL Rushing Touchdown Leader—1991—

NFL Offensive Rookie of The Year—1989

Barry Sanders Career Rushing Yards—15,269—

Barry Sanders Career Yards Per-Carry average—5.0

Sanders was selected to the 1990's All-Decade Team

Detroit Lions Number 20 Was retired

Barry Sanders won The Heisman Trophy— 1988—

Maxwell award—1988—

Walter Camp Award—1988—

Unanimous All-America—1988

Barry Sanders was Inducted into The NFL Pro Football Hall of Fame in 2004

On this day in Sports History, January 9, 1934 Bryan Bartlett Starr was born in Montgomery Alabama

Although Bart Starr was not drafted very high he became one of the most prolific quarterbacks in the history of the NFL

Highlights of Bart Starr's NFL career

Bart Starr was the only Quarterback to win 5 League Championship until Tom Brady tied this record in 2016.—Not to take anything away from Brady or Starr but isn't it a coincidence that Brady and Starr played for two of the greatest coaches in NFL history

Bart Starr was drafted by The Green Bay Packers in 1956 in the 17ᵗʰ round and was picked number 200.

Starr played for Green Bay from 1956—1971

Starr led the Packers to The NFL championships 5 times—1961—1962—1965—1966—1967

Bart Starr was the quarterback that won the first 2 Super Bowls

Starr was the Most valuable player in both of the first 2 Super Bowls

He was selected to the Pro Bowl 4 times—1960—1961—1962—1966

Starr was selected First Team All-Pro—1966

Second Team All-Pro 2 Times—1962—1964

Bart Starr was the NFL Most Valuable Player—1966—

The NFL Passer Rating Leader 5 times—1962—1964—1966—1968—1969—

He was selected to The NFL 1960s All Decade Team

Bart Starr is in the Green Bay Packers Hall of Fame-

Green Bay Packers Jersey Number 15 has been retired

In his career at Green Bay he Attempted 3,149 passes and he completed 1,808 for a passing of 57.4—Per-cent.

He ended up with a total of 24,718 Passing yards.

Bart Starr ended up with a Passing rating of 80.5

Bryan Bartlett "Bart" Starr Was inducted t\into the Green Bay Packers Hall of Fame and the NFL Football Hall of Fame in 1977.

CHAPTER 5

ON THIS DAY IN SPORTS
HISTORY BASKETBALL

In 1950 Earl Lloyd was the first African American to play in the NBA one year after the National Basketball Association was created in 1949.

On this day in Sports History, February 28, 1998, The Indiana Pacers beat Portland by the score of 124-59; This was the first time in NBA history that one team beat another by more than twice the score.

On this day in Sports History, June 8, 2018 The Golden State Warriors won The NBA Championship over the Cleveland Cavaliers

On this day in Sports History February 28, 1998 when Indiana Pacers Defeated the Portland Trailblazers by the score of 124 to 59, it was the first time in NBA that a team beat another by more than twice the score.

On this day in Sports History July 2, 2018, LeBron James signed a contract to play for the Los Angeles Lakers. This came about just after the Cleveland Cavaliers lost the NBA Championship to the Golden State Warriors. The Contract is worth 154 million dollars for 4 years.

On this day in Sports History June 9, 2018, The Golden State Warriors won the NBA champion ship by defeating the Cleveland Cavaliers in 4 games.

Ray G. Claveran

The scores were; Game 1 played in Oakland; Golden State won by the score of 124-114 in overtime—

Game 2 played in Oakland; Golden State won by the score of 122-103

Game 3 played in Cleveland, Golden State won by the score of 110-102

Game 4 played in Cleveland, Golden State won by the score of 108-85.— (it's called a sweep)

On this day in Sports History June 3, 2018 in game 2 of the NBA finals against the Cleveland Cavaliers. Seth Curry set a new NBA record for the Most 3 point scores in an NBA finals game. Seth Curry scored 9 three pointers to set the record.

CHAPTER 6

• • • • • • • • • • • • • • • • • • •

A FEW LEGENDS IN BASKETBALL

On this day in Sports History October 14, 1910 John Wooden was born in Hall Indiana

On this day in Sports History June 4, 2010 John Wooden died

Highlights of John Wooden's career as a Coach and as a Player.

John Wooden, Nicked Named the Wizard of Westwood because of his Streak of Seven consecutive NCAA Championships in a row, and 10 Championships in a12 year period as the coach at NCLA.

Wooden coached at Indiana State—1946—1948

He coached Baseball for 2 years at Indiana State—1946—1948

He coached at UCLA for 27 years from1948—1975—

At UCLA Wooden coached UCLA teams to the NCAA Regional Final Four—12 times—1964— 1965—1966 —1967—1968—1969—1970 —1971—1972—1973—1974—1975—

John Wooden coached The UCLA Bruins to The NCAA Division 1 Tournament Championship 10 times—1964—1965—1967—1968—1969 —1970—1971—1972—1973—1975—

John Wooden' UCLA Teams won The NCAA Division 1 Championship an amazing 7 Times in a row—1967—1968—1969—1870—1971—1972—1973.

Wooden was named AP College Coach of the Year—5 times—1967 —1969—1970—1972—1973—

Wooden was awarded The Henry LBA Award—7 times—1964— 1967—1969—1970—1971—1972—1973—

He was named NABC Coach of the Year—5 times—1964—1967— 1969—1970—1972—

John Wooden was received The Presidential Medal of Freedom—2003

As a player John Wooden was selected as a Consensus All American 3 times—1930—1931—1932—

NBL Scoring Leader—1933—

John Wooden was The Helms Player of the Year—1932—

John Wooden was on the NBL First Team 1938

ᏬᎳᎳᎩ

The Following are a few Quote by John Wooden

Things turn out best for people who make the best of the way things turn out. John Wooden 1910—2010

What you are as a person is far more important than what you are as a basketball player. John Wooden 1910—2010

The main ingredient of stardom is the rest of the team. John Wooden 1910—2010

Talent is god given. Be humble. Fame is man-given. Be grateful. Conceit is self-given. Be careful John Wooden 1910—2010

Material possessions, winning scores and great reputations are meaningless in the eyes of the lord, because he knows what we really are and that's all that matters. John Wooden 1910—2010

Consider the rights of others before your own feelings, and the feelings of others before your own rights. John Wooden 1910—2910

Do not let what you cannot do interfere with what you can do. John Wooden 1910—2010

Success comes from knowing that you did your best to become the best that you are capable of becoming. John Wooden 1910—2010

Success is never final, failure is never fatal. It's courage that counts. John Wooden 1910—2010

Be more concerned with your character than your reputation because your character is what you really are, while your reputation is merely what others think you are. John Wooden 1910—2010

Be prepared to be honest. John Wooden 1910—2010

If you're not making mistakes, then you are not doing anything. I'm positive that a doer makes mistakes. John Wooden 1910—2010

A coach is someone who can give correction without causing resentment. John Wooden 1910—2010

Ability is a poor man's wealth. John Wooden 1910—2010

Don't measure yourself by what you have accomplished, but by what you should have accomplished with your ability. John Wooden. 1910—2010

Failure is not fatal, but failure to change might be. John Wooden 1910—2010

I'd rather have a lot of talent and a little experience than a lot of experience t and a little talent. John Wooden 1910—2010

If you don't have time to do it right, when will you have time to do it over. John Wooden 1910—2010

It isn't what you do, but how you do it. John Wooden 1910—2010

It's not important who starts the game but who finishes it. John Wooden 1910—2010

It's the details that are vital. Little things make big things happen. John Wooden 1910—2010

It's what you learn after you know it all that counts. John Wooden 1910—2010

Never mistake activity for achievement. John Wooden 1910—2010

Winning takes talent, to repeat takes character. John Wooden 1910—2010

You can't live a perfect day without doing something for someone who will never be able to repay you. John Wooden 1910—2010

John Wooden was inducted into the basketball Hall of Fame as a player in 1960

Wooden was inducted into the Basketball Hall of Fame as a coach in 1973

If you are in search for a good role mole for your children there it is!

☙✦❧

On this day in sports History, December 7, 1956 Larry Joe Bird was born in West Baden Springs, Indiana

Highlights of Larry Birds NBA Basketball career

Larry Bird had one of the most amazing Basketball Careers in the history of the game. He was an outstanding college player —an outstanding player in the NBA— An outstanding Coach in the NBA — and an outstanding executive in the NBA. (Now how is that for a career in sports?) Bird is the only man in NBA history to be named— Most valuable Player—Coach of the year—and Executive of the year. Larry Bird was also named National College Player of The Year—1979

Bird was drafted by the Boston Celtics in the first round and was the sixth player to be picked. He played in the NBA from 1979—1992.

He was the coach for the Indiana Pacers 4 times—1997—1998—1999—2000

Bird and his Boston Celtics Team mates won the NBA championship 3 times—1981—1984—1986

Larry Bird was selected the NBA finals MVP— 2 times. —1984—1986

He was an NBA All Star. —12 times—1980—1981—1982—1983— 1984—1985—1986—1987—1988—1990—1991—1992

He was named the MVP in the All Star Game—1982

He was the NBA Most Valuable Player— 3 times—1984—1985—1986—

Larry Bird was All NBA First Team— 9 times—1980—1981—1982— 1983—1984—1985—1986—1987—1988—

He was All NBA Second Team—1990

He was All Defensive Second Team— 3 times—1982—1983—1984

He was selected Rookie of the Year 1980

He was the 3 point shooting champion— 3 times—1986—1987—1988—

He was selected to the 50-40-90 Club—2 times —1987—1988—

Larry Bird was selected by the AP as the Athlete of the Year—1986—

Bird was selected to the NBA's 50th anniversary ALL Time Team

Larry Birds Jersey, Number 33 was retired by the Boston Celtics

Larry Bird had a very impressive College career as well.

He was the College Player of the Year—1979

Consensus First Team All American— 2 times—1978—1979

He was selected to the Third Team ALL American by NABC—UPI—1977

He was MVC Player of the Year— 2 times—1978—1979

Bird was selected the NBA Coach of the Year—1998—

He was the Head Coach for the All Star Game—1998

Larry Bird was the NBA's Executive of the Year—2012

Larry birds Career Statistics In the NBA

Bird scored a total of—21,791 points—

Bird averaged —24.3 per game

Bird had a total of 5,695Assists—for a 6.1 average per game.

He had a total of —8,974—Rebounds for a10.0 average per game

Larry Bird was on the team representing the United States in the Word University games.

The team won the Gold Medal in Sofia —1977

World International tournament in the United States—1978 won the Gold Medal

Larry Bird was on The Olympic Team that won the Gold Medal in Barcelona— 1992—

Larry Joe Bird was inducted into the Naismith Memorial Basketball Hall of Fame in 1998—

Bird was inducted again into the Basketball Hall of Fame as a member of the Dream Team in 2010

On this day in Sports History, February 17, 1963 Michael Jeffrey Jordan was born In Brooklyn New York

Highlights of Michael Jordan's Basketball career

Jordan had an outstanding college career at North Carolina from 1981-1984.

In 1982 Jordan led North Carolina to the NCAA National Championship

He was consensus First Team All American— 2 times—1983—1984

Jordan was The ACC Player of the Year—1984

His Jersey number 23 was retired by the University of North Carolina

Ray G. Claveran

He was USA Basketball Male Athlete of the Year—2 times —1983-1984

Michael Jordan is considered by many as the greatest basketball player of all time. Not only was he a great player he was also the most exciting basketball player to ever play in the NBA,

Jordan was the 3rd player picked in the first round by the Chicago Bull in 1984,.

Jordan Played for the Bulls from 1984-1993—From 1995—1998——

Jordan played for The Washington Wizards from201— 2003

Jordan and the Bulls won the NBA Championship—6 times—1991—1992—1993—1996—1997—1998—

Jordan was selected Rookie of the Year—1985

He was selected to the NBA All Rookie First Team—1985

Jordan was the NBA finals MVP—6 times—1991—1992—1993—1996—1997—1998—

He was the NBA Most Valuable Player —5 times—1988—1991—1992—1996—1998—

Michael Jordan was an NBA All Star— 14 times—1985—1986—1987—1988—1989—1990—1991—1992—1993—1996—1997—1998—2002—2003

He was MVP in the NBA All Star Game— 3 times—1988—1996—1998—

Jordan was on the All NBA First Team— 10 Times— 1987—1988—1989—1990—1991—1992—1993— 1996—1997—1998—

He was on the All NBA Second Team—1985

MJ (Nickname) was Defensive Player of the Year—1988

Michael Jordan was selected to the NBA All Defensive First Team— 9 times—1988—1989—1990—1991—1992—1993—1996—1997—1998—

Michael Jordan was the NBA Scoring Champion— 10 times—1987—1988— 189—1990—1991—1992—1993—1996—1997—1998— (

Jordan was the NBA Steals Leader— 3 times—1988—1990—1993

He was the NBA Slam Dunk Contest winner —2 times—1997—1998—

Jordan was the AP Athlete of the Year— 3 times—1991—1992—1993

Michael Jordan scored —32,292 points in his NBA career

Jordan averaged —30.1 points per game in his NBA career.

He had —6,672 rebounds

Michael Jordan Had an average of —6.2 rebounds per game.

He had—5,633 Assists

Jordan averaged —5.3 Assists per game

Jordan and Team mates won the Gold medal at The Olympics in Los Angeles—1984— and again in Barcelona in—1992

FIBA American Championships Jordan and Team mates won the gold Medal in Portland —1992

The Pan American Games in Caracas—He was on the team that won the Gold Medal.

He was chosen by Sports Illustrated as the Sportsperson of the Year— 1991

Jordan was elected to the NBA 50th anniversary All Time Team

Michael Jordan is the Principle owner, and chairman of the Charlotte Hornets in the NBA

Michael Jordan became the first NBA Player in history to become a Billionaire. He is the third richest African American behind Oprah Winfrey, and Robert F, Smith.

Michael Jeffrey Jordan was inducted into the Basketball Hall of Fame in 2009 as a Player in the NBA

In 2010 he was inducted again as a member of the 1992 Dream Team that won the Gold Medal for the United States in the Olympics in Barcelona Spain

He was also inducted into the FIBA Hall of Fame

On This day in Sports History, May 28, 1938 Jerry Alan West was born in Chelyan West Virginia.

Highlights of Jerry West's NBA Basketball career

Jerry West became on of the greatest basketball players in NBA history. When you see the NBA LOGO, It is Jerry West's Silhouette you are looking at. (How is that for an honor to be proud of).

Jerry West was drafted by the Minneapolis Lakers In 1960. The Lakers moved to Los Angeles, Jerry West played his entire career with the Lakers.

West was chosen in the first round and was the second player picked. (and what a career he had.)

The season before he joined the NBA he led the West Virginia Mountaineers to the

NCAA Championship Game in 1959, despite the loss he was chosen the final four, Most Outstanding Player.

West was the scoring champion—1970—

West scored —25,192—

West had a scoring average of 27 points per game

He had— 6,238 Assists—

West had —5,356 Rebounds

NBA Champions—1972

NBA A[[-Star Game— most Valuable Player—1972

All-NBA Second Team— 2 Times— 1968—1969

All-NBA First team—10 times—1962—1963—1964—1965—1966—1967—1970—1971—1972—1973—

NBA finals—Most Valuable Player—1969—

NBA All-Star—14 times 1961—1974—

NBA Assist Leader—1972—

NBA All-Defensive First Team—4 times—1970—1971—1972—1973

NBA All-Defensive second team —1969—

NBA 35th Anniversary Team—

NBA 50th Anniversary Team—

Number 44 of the Los Angeles Lakers is retired—

Jerry West coached the Lakers from 1976—1979—

As an executive; NBA Championships—8 times—1980—1982—1985—1987—1988—2000—2015—2017—

NBA Executive of the year—2 times 1995—2004

West was on the U.S. team that won the gold medal at the Pan -Am games played in Chicago—1959

West was Co- Captain — on the U.S. Olympic team played in Rome — The team won the Gold Medal—1960—The team was inducted into the Naismith Memorial Hall of Fame In 2010.

Jerry Alan West was inducted into the Naismith Basketball Hall of Fame in 1980

On this day in Sports History August 21, 1936 Wilton Norman Chamberlain was born in Philadelphia, Pennsylvania

On this day in Sports History, October 12, 1999 Wilton Norman Chamberlain died.

Highlights of Wilt Chamberlain's NBA Career

Wilt was drafted by the Philadelphia Warriors in 1959—

He played in the NBA from 1959—1973 He played Center and wore number 13.

Chamberlain coached the San Diego Conquistadors from —1973—1974

Chamberlain played for the Harlem Globetrotters 2 years —1958—1959

Philadelphia/ San Francisco Warriors—1959—1965—

Wilt played for the Philadelphia 76ers —1965—1968—

Chamberlain played for the Los Angeles Lakers 1968—1973—

As a rookie in the NBA Chamberlain was 7' 1" tall and weighed in at just about 250 pounds.

Chamberlain was voted Rookie of The Year—1960

He was the NBA scoring champion— 7 times —1960—1961—1962—1963—1964—1965—1966—

He was the NBA rebounding leader —11 times—1960—1961—1962—1963—1966—1967—1968—1969—1971—1972—1973—

He was the NBA Assist Leader —1968

NBA Champions two times —1967, with Philadelphia—

1972, with the Los Angeles Lakers

NBA Finals Most Valuable Player —1972

NBA Most Valuable Player —4 Times—1960—1966—1967—1968

NBA All Star— 13 times—1960—1961—1962—1963—1964—1965—1966—1967—1968—1969—1971—1972—1973

The following are NBA records Chamberlain had at the end of his career

Wilt Chamberlain is the only player in NBA history to score **100 points in a single game**

He is the only player in NBA history to average 30 points and 20 rebounds per game, and <u>he did this for his entire career!</u>

He has the highest single season scoring average—50.4 points per game.

He set the single game rebounding record of —55

He set the single season rebounding average of—27.2

Chamberlain had the single season rebounding record of —2,149

He set the single season scoring record of —4,029

Chamberlain se the record for the most minutes played per game average of 48 ½ min. per game. (whew!)

In his career Wilt he scored— 31,419 points,

Wilt Chamberlain had an average of— 30 points per game

Chamberlain had— 23,924 Rebounds

Wilt Chamberlain had an average of—22.9 Rebounds per game.

Wilt Chamberlain was the MVP at the NBA All Star Game in 1960

He was All NBA First Team —7 times—1960—1961—1962—1964—1965—1966—1968

All NBA Second Team 3 times—1963—1965—1972—

Chamberlain was All NBA Defensive Team —2 times—1972—1973—

Chamberlain Made the NBA-35ᵗʰ Anniversary Team—

He was chosen to the 50ᵗʰ NBA Anniversary Team

He was chosen as the NCAA Final Four Most Outstanding Player —1957

Chamberlain was a First Team All American—2 times 1957—1958—

Wilt Chamberlains Jersey, Number 13 was retired by the Golden State Warriors—

His jersey was retires by the Philadelphia 76ers—

His Jersey was retired by the Los Angeles Lakers —

His Jersey was retired by the University Of Kansas

Wilt Norman Chamberlain was inducted into The Naismith Memorial Basketball Hall of Fame in 1978

On This Day in Sports History April 16 1941, Ferdinand Lewis Alcindor was born—He is better known as Kareem Abdul-Jabbar. He was born in New York City, New York

Highlights Kareem Abdul Jabbar Basketball career

Kareem Abdul-Jabbar played his college Basketball for UCLA and was coached by one of the very best coaches in sports history—Bill Wooden.

At the end of his playing career at UCLA he held many records for College Basketball

Kareem led the UCLA Bruins to 3 Consecutive NCAA Championships —1967—1968—1969

Kareem Abdul-Jabbar was selected the NCAA final four Most Outstanding Player —3 times—1967—1968—1968

He was the National College Player of the year—3 times—1967—1968—1969—

Kareem was consensus First Team All American—3 times—1967—1968—1969

Number 33 was retired by UCLA.

He had the highest career scoring average of 26.4 —

The most points in a single game—61 points—February 25, 1967

He had the most career field goals —943— (He is tied with Don Maclean for this record)

Abdul-Jabbar scored the most points in a season—870 in 1967.

He had the highest season scoring average of— 29 points in 1967

He scored the most field goals in a season—346—1967

He also had the most free throw attempts in a season—271 —1967

Kareem Abdul-Jabbar was inducted into the College Basketball Hall of Fame in 2006

Wow what a college career!!!

Kareem Abdul-Jabbar's NBA career achievements and awards'

Kareem Abdul-Jabbar was drafted by the Milwaukee Bucks In 1969, he was the first player picked in the 1969 NBA draft.

He played 20 years when he retired in 1989. He played for Milwaukee from 1969—1975—

Kareem Jabbar played for the Los Angeles Lakers from 1975—1989

He was listed at 7ft. 2 inches and weighed approximately 225 pounds.

Kareem played the center position,

He wore number 33 on his jersey

Kareem Abdul-Jabbar was the Rookie of the year in 1970

Kareem Abdul-Jabbar was selected to the All NBA First Team—10 times—1971—1972—1973—1974—1976—1977—1980—1981—1984 —1986—

He was All NBA Second Team—5 times—1970—1978—1979—1983— 1985—

Kareem was an NBA All Star—19 times—1970—1977—1979—1989—

NBA Champions—6 times—1971—1980—1982—1985—1987—1988-

Kareem was the NBA MVP—6 times—1971—1972—1974—1976— 1977—1980—

He was voted NBA finals MVP— 2 times—1971—1985—

He was the NBA Scoring Champion— 2 times—1971—1972—

Kareem Abdul-Jabbar was not only an offensive threat; he was also a great defensive player as well.

Abdul-Jabbar-was on the NBA All Defensive First Team— 5 times— 1974—1975—1979—1980—1981—

He was on the NBA All Defensive Second Team—6 times—1970— 1971—1976—1978—1984—

He was the NBA Rebounding Champion—1976—

Kareem was the NBA Block Shot Leader—4 times—1975— 1976—1979—1980—

Kareem Abdul-Jabbar was selected to the NBA All Time Team

His jersey, Number 33 was retired by the Milwaukee Bucks—

Number 33 was also retired by the Los Angeles Lakers

These are a few of His NBA career accomplishments—

Blocked Shots—3.189—5 blocked shots per game average

Points scored 38.387—24.6 points per game average

Rebounds—17.440 —11.2 per game verage!

Kareem Abdul-Jabbar was inducted into the Naismith National Basketball Hall of Fame in 1994

CHAPTER 7

● ● ● ● ● ● ● ● ● ● ● ● ● ● ● ● ● ● ● ●

ON THIS DAY IN SPORTS HISTORY GOLF

On this day in Sports History Sunday,September 30, 2018 Europe Beat the United State to win Ryder Cup, the tournament was held in Europe at Le Golf National Near Paris

On this day in Sports History Sunday, July 23, 2018 Francisco Molinari became the first Italian to win the British Open Molinari won the tournament by 2 strokes. The event was held at Carnoustie, in Scotland.

On this day in Sports History, July 12, 2018 BrooksKoepkawon the PGA Championship. The win was worth $ 1.980,000. for first place— Not to bad for 4 days work!

On this day in Sports History, April 13, 1986 Jack Nicklaus won a record sixth Masters Tournament and Making him the oldest winner of the Masters Tournament at 46, the win was the 70th win on the PGA Tour

On this day in Sports History, April, 13, 2003 Canadian Mike Weir won The Masters

On this day in Sports History, April 12, 1964 Arnold Palmer became the First 4 time winner of The Masters Golf Tournament.

On this day in Sports History, April 9,1950Jimmy De Maret won the Masters for the 3rd time

On This day in Sports History, April 15, 1984 Ben Crenshaw wins The Masers for the first time

On this day in Sports History, June!0, 1977 Allan Geiberger shot a 59 At The Danny Thomas Memphis Classic, he won the tournament

On this day in Sports History October 12, 1991 Chip Beck shot a 59 at the Las Vegas Invitational in the third round he ended up tied for third in the tournament

On this day in sports History January 24 1999 David Duval a 59 in the final round to win the Bob Hope Classic

On this day in sports history September 13, 2013 Jim Furyk Shot a 12 under par 59 at the BMW Championship he came in third in the tournament

On this day in Sports History July 8 2010 Paul Goydos shot a 12 under Par 59 at The John Deer Classic, He came in second in the tournament

On this day in Sports History, August 1, 2016 Stuart Appleby shot an 11 under par 59 in the final round to win the tournament

On this day in Sports History, August 7, 2016 Jim Furyk shot an 11 under par 58 at the Travelers Championship, He came in tied for fifth in the tournament

On this day in Sports History June 10, 2018 Dustin Johnson Eagles the 18th hole and won the St. Jude Classic and reclaims the number 1 Ranking in the world..

On this day in Sports History July 8, 2018, Sei Young Kim set a new record on the LPGA by winning the Thornberry creek LPGA Classic in an amazing 31 under par. She broke the record of 27 under by 4 strokes. The LPGA was founded in 1950 and I believe the record will last another 68 years or more. Her scores were; 63—65—64—65—

Golfers that have won at least 6 Majors

Jack Nicklaus—6 Masters—4 US Opens—3 The Open (British) —

5—PGA Championships—Total—18

Tiger Woods—4 Masters—3 US Opens—3 the Open (British)

—4 PGA Championships—Total—14

Walter Hagen—0 Masters—2 Us Opens—4 the Open (British)

5 PGA Championships—Total—11

Ben Hogan—2 Masters—4 US Opens—1 The Open (British)—

2 PGA Championships—Total—9

Gary Player—3 Masters—1 US Open—3 The Open (British)

2—PGA Championships—Total—9

Tom Watson—2 Masters—1 US Open—5—The Open (British)

0 PGA Championships—Total—8

Gene Sarazen—1 Master—2 US Opens—1The Open (British)

3—PGA Championships—Total—7

Arnold Palmer—4 Masters—1 US Open--2--The Open (British)-0

PGA Championships—Total—7

Sam Snead—3 Masters—0 US Open—1The Open (British)

3 PGA Championships—Total 7

Bobby Jones—0 Masters—4 US Opens—3 The Open (British)

O PGA championships—Total—7

Harry Vardon—0 Masters—1 US Open—6 The Open (British)

0 PGA Championships—Total—7

Lee Trevino—0 Masters—2 US Opens—2 The Open (British)

2 PGA Championships—Total—6

Nick Faldo—3 Masters—0 US Opens—3The Open (British)

0 PGA Championships—Total—6

The Players that have won the most Masters

Jack Nicklaus has won the most Masters—6

Tiger woods has won 4 Masters

Arnold Palmer has won 4 Masters

Gary Player Has won 3 Masters

Sam Snead has won 3 Masters

Phil Mickelson has won 3 Masters

Nick Faldo has won 3 Masters

The Players that Have won the most US Opens

Jack Nicklaus Has won 4 US Opens

Ben Hogan has won 4 US Opens

Bobby Jones has won 4 US Opens

Tiger Woods has won 3 US Opens

Walter Hagen has won 2 US Opens

Lee Trevino has won 2 US Opens

Gene Sarazen has won 2 US Opens

Players that have won the most British Opens

Harry Vardon has won 6 British Opens

Tom Watson has won 5 British Opens

James Braid has won 5 British Opens

John Henry Taylor has won5 British Opens

Peter Thompson has won 5 British Open

Players that have won the most PGA Championships

Jack Nicklaus has won 5 PGA Championships

Walter Hagen has won 5 PGA Championships

Tiger Woods has won 4 PGA Championships

Gene Sarazen has won 3 PGA Championships

Sam Snead has won 3 PGA Championships

CHAPTER 8

● ● ● ● ● ● ● ● ● ● ● ● ● ● ● ● ● ● ●

A FEW LEGENDS IN GOLF

On this day in Sports History, Jack William Nicklaus was born January21 1940—In Columbus, Ohio

He married to Barbara Bash in1960.

Nicklaus turned Professional in 1961 and retired in2005 He played on the PGA tour and retired from the Champions tour.(Senior Tour)

Jack Nicklaus (The golden bear) as he is known is considered by most as the greatest golfer that has ever lived. If you look up his tournament wins on tour; and especially his wins in the four majors there is no doubt.

The amazing thing is that he won 18 majors; he came in second 19 times

As a matter of fact his first tour win was in 1962 in one of the four majors, the U S Open when he defeated the great Arnold Palmer in the 18 hole- play-off by 3 stokes.

Jack Nicklaus is not only a great golfer of years past; Jack Nicklaus Has been a great ambassador for the Game of golf.

As a life member of the P.G.A, I am proud to say thank you Mr. Nicklaus

I can not say for certain, but if memory serves me right I recall reading that after every tournament Jack Nicklaus played in he would send a letter to the golf course that he played and would thank the host Professional for his efforts, he would thank the golf course superintendent and tell him the course was in great shape.

Now if this is not 100% true then I just started a great rumor

Highlights of Jack Nicklaus's career in Golf

On the PGA tour he won— 73 times—third most all time

On the PGA tour of Australasia he won— 7 times

PGA Champions tour he won— 10 times

Other—19 times—Other seniors he won—8 times

Jack Nicklaus has won a record 18 Majors

Nicklaus won The Masters —6 times—1963—1965—1966—1972—1975—1986

Nicklaus won The US Open— 4 times—1962—1967—1972 —1980

Nicklaus won The Open Championship— 3 times—1966—1970—1978

Nicklaus won the PGA —5 times—1963—1971—1973—1975—1980

Jack Nicklaus was the PGA Leading Money Winner— 8 times—1964 —1965—1967—1971—1972—1973—1975—1976

Jack Nicklaus was the PGA Player of the Year —5 times—1967—1972—1973—1975—1976

Nicklaus received the Bob Jones Award in—1975—

Jack Nicklaus was awarded The Payne Stewart Award in—2000—

He received The PGA Tour Lifetime Achievement Award—2008—

Jack Nicklaus received The Congressional Gold Medal in—2015

Jack William Nicklaus was inducted into the World Golf Hall of Fame in—1974

On this day in Sports History, December 30ᵗʰ 1975; Eldrick Tont Woods was born in Cypress California. He is better known as; Tiger Woods throughout the golf world.

There is a good argument on both sides as to who is the greatest golfer of all time between Tiger Woods or Jack Nicklaus. I know that Tiger was the most exiting player that I ever watched

Highlights of Tigers Woods career

Tiger woods was rookie of the year— 1996

Tiger won a total of 139 Professional Tournaments

Woods won 79 PGA Tour Tournaments— (Second All Time)

Tiger won 40 European Tour tournaments— (Third All Time)

Japan Golf Tour—2—

Asian Tour—1—

PGA Tour of Australasia—1

Other—16—

Tiger Woods won 14 Majors, second to Jack Nicklaus

He won The Masters —4 times—1997—2001—2002—2005

He won the US Open—3 times—2000—2002—2008

He won The Open Championship—3 times—2000—2005—2006

He won The PGA Championship 4 times—1999—2000—2006—2007

Tiger Woods was PGA Tour Player of the Year—A record— 11 times—1997—1999—2000—2001—2002—2003—2005—2006—2007—2009—2013

Tiger was the PGA Tour Leading Money Winner—A record —10 times—1997—1999—2000—2001—2002—2005—2006—2007—2009—2013

Woods won The Vardon Trophy—9 times—1999—2000—2001—2002—2003—2005—2007—2009—2013

He won The Byron Nelson Award—A record— 9 times—1999—2000—2001—2002—2003—2005—2006—2007—2009

Woods was the Fed-Ex Cup Champion—2 times—2007—2009

Tiger Woods held the Number one golfer in the world for the most consecutive weeks and he also holds the record for the most total weeks as the Worlds number one player. Woods was the Number One Player for a total of 683 weeks

On this day in Sports History, September 10, 1929 Arnold Daniel Palmer was born in Latrobe Pennsylvania he passed away on September 25, 2016.

Palmer was married in 1954 to Winifred Walzer until her death in1999. He married again in 2005 to Kathleen Gawthrop, until his death in 2016

Arnie as he was called was also known as, "The king"

His millions of loyal fans were known as; Arnie's Army.

I can not think of any other athlete in any sport that was loved and respected more by his peers and his fans than Arnold Palmer, "The king:

Highlights of Arnold Palmer's career

Arnold Palmer turned professional in 1954 and retired 52 years later in2006

Arnold Palmer won 7 Majors

He won the Masters—4 times—1959—1960—1962—1964—

Palmer won the— US Open—One time—1960

Palmer won The Open Championship 2 times—1961—1962

Palmer won a total of 95 professional Tournaments

Arnold Palmer won 62 PGA Tour Tournaments

He won 2 times on the European tour

Palmer won ten times in the PGA Champions Tour;,5 of the 10 wins on the Senior Tour were Senior Major Championships

He won the PGA Seniors Championship —3 times—1980—1984—1985-

He won the Seniors US Open —1 time—1981

He won the PGA Seniors Championship —1 Time—1984

Palmer won 16 other professional Golf Tournaments

Palmer also won 5 other Senior Tour events.

Arnold Palmer was the PGA Leading Money Winner—4 times—1958—1960—1962—1963

He was the PGA Player of The Year—2 times—1960—1963

Palmer won the Vardon Trophy—4 times—1961—1962—1964—1967--

Arnold Palmer was Sports Illustrated Sportsman of The Year—1 time—1960

Bob Jones Award—1 time—1971The Old Tom Morris Award—1 time—1983

PGA Tour Lifetime Achievement Award—1 time 1998

Payne Stewart Award—1 time—2000

Presidential Medal of Freedom—1 time 2004—

Congressional gold Medal—1 time—2009

I guarantee you one thing: statistics can never measure the quality of a man.

To my way of thinking; The King was the most successful golfer of All Time. When I think of Arnold Palmer I think of kindness

Arnold Daniel Palmer was inducted into the World Golf Hall of Fame in 1974

On this day in Sports History August 13, 1912 William Ben Hogan was born in Stephenville Texas.

Ben Hogan died on July 27, 1997 at the age of 84 Ben Hogan was the youngest of three children born to Clara and Chester Hogan, Ben's Father committed suicide in the family Home when Hogan was close to 9 years old, Ben Hogan was home at the time.

Highlights of Ben Hogan career

Hogan had 3 Nicknames that were perfect for is personality; one was Bantam Ben One was The Hawk and the other The Wee Iceman.

Bantam Ben; this nickname was given to Ben Hogan because of his ability to hit the golf-ball past most of the much larger players on the PGA Tour. Hogan was only 5 feet 8 inches tall and weighed 145 pounds.

The Hawk and The Wee Iceman was a tribute to Hogan for his ability to concentrate so well while playing in a golf tournament.

Ben Hogan turned professional in 1930; he was born in 1912 which means when he turned professional he was 18 years old.

Hogan retired from golf in 1971,

Ben Hogan retired with 69 professional wins.

He won 64on the PGA Tour which is 4th all time.

Ben Hogan won 9 Major Championships

He won The Masters—2 times—1951—1953

Hogan won the US Open—4 times—1948—1950—1951—1953

Ben Hogan won The Open Championship—1 time—1953

Hogan won the PGA Championship. -2 times—1946—1948

Ben Hogan was the PGA Tour Leading Money Winner.—5 times—1940—1941—1942—1946—1948

Hogan was the PGA Player of The Year—4 times—1948—1950—1951—1953—

Ben Hogan won The Vardon Trophy—3 times—1940—1941—1948

Hogan was The Associated Press Male Athlete of The Year1953

Bantam Ben Hogan was inducted unto The World Golf Hall of Fame In 1974

On this day in Sports History, March 17, 1902 Robert Tyre Jones Jr. was Born in Atlanta Georgia

On this day in Sports History December 18, 1971 Bobby Jones died at the age of 69 In Atlanta Georgia

Highlights of Bobby Jones Golf Career

I have been A Member of the PGA since 1974 and I had never heard this story and I have asked several golf professionals if they have heard this one and so far none have

The story goes that in 1930 Before the first tournament of the Majors Bob Jones made a bet with the British Bookmakers that he would win the four majors with the odds at 50 to1; He did and he won over 60,000 dollars.—Did you know that???

The Most amazing thing about bobby Jones as a golfer is the fact that he was an amateur and played against the best professional of his time.

Bob Jones won 13 major Championships

In1934, 4 years after he retired from competitive golf he played in the Masters, which he co-founded and placed 13th.

Bobby Jones won The US Open—4 times—1923—1926—1929—1930

Jones won The Open Championship—3 times—1926—1927—1930

Bob Jones did not play in The PGA Championship—

Bobby   Jones   won   The   US   Amateur—5
times—1924—1925—1927—1928—1930

Bobby Jones won the British Amateur —1 time1930

He was awarded The James E. Sullivan Award—1 time—1930

Bob Jones was inducted into The Georgia Tech Athletic Hall of Fame
in 1958

He was also inducted into The Georgia Tech Engineering Hall of fame
in 1997

Bob Jones won his first golf tournament when he was either 5 or six

About the same age I was when I was getting Potty Trained

**Bobby Jones was inducted into The World Golf Hall Of Fame in 1974.
(And he well damned deserved it0**

**On this day in Sports History December I, 1939 Lee Buck Trevino
was born in Dallas Texas**

Lee was also known as "The Merry Mex," and "Supermex"

Lee Trevino Is considered by many as one of the greatest golfers of all
time.

Trevino is without a doubt the greatest Hispanic Golfer in history of
golf.

Myself being of Mexican Heritage I am especially Proud of Lee Trevino.

Highlights of Lee Trevino's career
Lee Trevino won 6 Major Championships

Lee Trevino Turned Professional in 1960 at the age of 21

Lee Trevino Top 10— 2 times—1975—1985

Lee Trevino won The US Open —2 times—1968—1971

Lee Trevino won The Open Championship—2 times 1971—1972

Lee won The PGA —2 times—1974—1984

Trevino had a total of 92 professional wins

Trevino won 29 PGA Tour Tournaments.(Tied for 19 all time)

He won 2 tournaments on the European Tour

Lee Trevino won I tournament on the Japanese Tour

He won 29 tournaments on the PGA Champions Tour (Seniors Tour)

3rd All Time

Other he won 21 times regular

Trevino also won 10 other Seniors Events

Lee Trevino was the PGA Tour Leading Money Winner—1 time—1970

Trevino won The Vardon Trophy —5 times— 1970—1971—1972—1974 —1980—

Trevino was the PGA Player of The Year—1 time—1971—

Trevino won The Jack Nicklaus Trophy—3 times—1990—1992—1994

On The Champions Tour

On the Champions Tour lee Trevino was The Rookie of The Year in 1990

Lee Trevino received The Arnold Palmer Award —2 times— 1990—1992

Trevino received The Byron Nelson Award—3 times—1990—1991—1992—

Trevino was The Sports Illustrated Sportsman of The Year—1 time—1971

Lee Trevino was The Associated Press Male Athlete of The Year—1 time—1971

Lee Buck Trevino was inducted into The World Golf Hall of Fame in 1981

CHAPTER 9

● ● ● ● ● ● ● ● ● ● ● ● ● ● ● ● ● ● ●

ON THIS DAY IN SPORTS HISTORY HOCKEY

On this day in Sports History May1 1893 Canada's governor General; Lord Stanley of Preston donated Hockey's Stanley Cup

On this day in Sports History August 9 1988 The Edmonton Oilers Traded Wayne Gretzky to the Los Angeles Kings Just about a month after he led the team to a Stanley Cup win

On this day in Sports History June 26, 2018 6 Players were nominated to joint the NHL Hall of Fame. The six Men will be inducted in November 2018. The Men and Lady nominated and their credentials for the Honor are as follows.

Martin Brodeur was born on May 6, 1972 in Montreal Quebec. He was a goalie with 691 wins and he had 125 shut-outs, He is one of only 15 Goalie's with more than 12 or more shut-outs in a single season

Martin St. Louis was born on June 18, 1975 in Laval Quebec. He was a Right Winger. St. Louis amassed 1033 points in 1134 games. St. Louis ranks in the top 75 scorers in NHL history. In 2004 he won the Hart Trophy as the MVP and the Ted Lindsay award as the outstanding Player.

Jayna Hefford was born May 14, 1977 in Trenton Ontario. She was a Right Winger. Jayna Hefford set records in Kingston minor hockey that have not been broken by Males or Female. She had a great playing college career at the University of Toronto. She became the first player in the Canadian Women's Hockey League to score 100 points. Jayna was a member of teams that won 4 Gold Medals for Canada in the Olympics, including the game winner against the United States in 2002.

Alexander Yakushev was born on January 2, 1947 in Moscow, Russia. He was a Left Winger. He was a star for the Soviet Union, Yakushev was a prolific scorer and for Moscow in the 1960's and 70's .He once scored 50 goals in a 44game league season. He coached Moscow Spartak and the Soviet National Team to Two Olympic Gold medals and 7 World Championships

Gary Bettman was born on June 2, 1952. Bettman will be inducted into the Hall of Fame as a Builder Gary Bettman is the longest serving Commissioner in any Professional Sport, he has been the Commissioner of the NHL since 1993. While the Commissioner the NHL has gone from 21 teams to 31, and generates 3 billion dollars U.S.

Willie O'Ree born on October 15, 1935 in Fredericton N.B. Willie O'Ree will be inducted into the NHL Hall of Fame in November 2018 as a Builder. Willie O'Ree has been called the Jackie Robinson of Hockey because he was the man that broke the color barrier in NHL Hockey. On January 18, 1958 he was called up to play for Boston against Montreal

On this day in Sports history Friday November 9, 2018,Commissioner, Gary Bateman—Martin Brodeur—Jayna Hefford—Willie O'Ree— Martin St Louis—and Alexander Yakushev were all inducted into the Hockey Hall of Fame.

On this day in Sports History June 7, 2018, The Washington Capitals won the Stanley Cup by defeating he Las Vegas Knights in 5 games. (Game 1; Las Vegas 6—Washington 4)—(Game 2; Washington 3—Vegas 2) (Game 3; Washington 3—Vegas 1)--(Game 4; Washington 6—Vegas 2)--(Game 5; Washington 4—Las Vegas 3)

What is amazing about the series is that Washington had never won the Stanley cup, AND IT WAS THE LAS VEGAS KNIGHTS FIRST YEAR IN THE NHL. It took Alex Ovechkin, the leader of the Capitals 13 years to finally win the Stanley Cup. Ovechkin was selected as the Most Valuable Player in the finals.

On this day in Sports History April 15 1989 Wayne Gretzky Playing for the Los Angeles Kings surpassed Gordie Howe's NH L scoring record of 1850. Gretzky retired in 1999 with 2857 Points.

On this day in Sports History December 28 1944 Maurice Richard became the first player to score 8 points in a NHL game. The Rocket had 5 goals and 3 assist in the Montreal Canadian 9-1 romp over Detroit.

On this day in Sports History March 18, 1945 Maurice Richard was the first player to score 50 goals in one season He did this in only 50 games

On this day in Sports History October the 8, 1992 The Ottawa Senators took the ice for the first NHL regular season game since leaving the league in 1934, The won the Game over the Montreal Canadians 5 to3

On this day in Sports History March 17, 2009 New Jersey goaltender Martin Brodeur set an NHL record with his 552 career regular season wins. The victory came in his 987 game, of a 15 year career played entirely with the New Jersey Devils. He surpassed Patrick Roy who had 551 wins in 1029 games. Martin Brodeur retired with 691 regular season wins

On this day in Sports History March 12, 1966 Bobby Hull playing for the Chicago Blackhawks became the first player in the NHL to score more than 50 goals in a season, getting his 51st goal against The New York Rangers. Hull was the highest scoring left wing in Hockey history with 1.018 goals and 2,017 points when he retired in 1980 at the age of 41.

On this day in Sports History, January 12, 1993 The Pittsburg Penguins stunned the Hockey World after announcing superstar Mario Lemieux has been diagnosed with Hodgkin's disease Lemieux immediately left the team to begin an intensive 5 week radiation treatment aimed at stopping the Cancer. Defying the odd, he returned to play six weeks later, after receiving his final radiation treatment that morning..Scoring at a torrid pace, he retook the points lead to win his second straight Art Ross Trophy, while guiding Pittsburg on a record-setting 17 game winning straight to finish first overall in the NHL.

On this day in Sports History September 15 1960 Montreal Canadian legend Maurice "Rocket" Richard announced his retirement after 18 years in the NHL. Known as one of the most intense players of his era, Richard was a prolific goal-scorer, leading the Canadians to eight Stanley Cup wins during his eighteen year career Richard was a cultural icon to Francophone Quebec Richard was honored as an inaugural members of the Order of Canada and was appointed to the Queen's Privy Council in 1992. In recognition of his achievements, The NHL Awards the Maurice "Rocket" Richard Trophy annually to the league's top goal- scorer during regular season play

On this day in Sports History May 2 1967 The Toronto Maple Leafs won their last Stanley Cup When the won the Sixth game 3-1 against the Montreal Canadians

On this day in Sports History September 15 1987 With 1 minute and 26 seconds left on the clock Mario Lemieux got a drop pas from team mate Wayne Gretzky and scored a goal over the glove of Soviet goalie Evgeni Belosheikin to give Canada a 6-5 lead in game 3In the Canada Cup finals. The tournament featured 2 of Hockey's greatest players Mario Lemieux and Wayne Gretzky. Wayne Gretzky set a new tournament record with 21 points and Mario was the top scorer in the tournament with 11 goals

On this day in Sports History, May 28, Hall of fame Goaltender, Patrick Roy Announced his retirement after 18 years in the league. Roy was on 4 Stanley Cup championship teams; He won 3 Conn Smythe Trophies as the MVP in the Play-offs

On this day in Sports History, June 11, 2012 The Los Angeles Kings won the Stanley Cey defeating the New Jersey Devils; 6 to1 in game 6. This was the first time an 8th seed won the Stanley Cup.

On this day in Sports History, June 9, 2010, Patrick Kane scored a goal for the Chicago Blackhawks in overtime to defeat the Philadelphia Flyers 4 to 3 in game 6. The Blackhawks had not won the Stanley Cup since 1961.

Stanley Cup Winners since 1993

(2018-Washington)—(2017--Pittsburg)—(2016-Pittsburg)—(2015—Chicago)—(2014-Los Angelese)--(2013-Chicago)—(2012 Los angeles)—(2011-Boston)--(2010-Chicago)—(2009-Pittsburg)—(2008-Detroit)-(2007-Anaheim)—(2006-Carolina)—(**2005-Season Cancelled)**—(2004-Tampa Bay)— (2003-New Jersey)-(2002-Detroit)—(2001-Colorado)—(2000-New Jersey)-(1999-Dallas)—(1998-Detroit)—(1997-Detroit) (1996Colorado)—(1995-New Jersey)—(1994-New York Rangers)—(1993-Montreal)

● ● ● ● ● ● ● ● ● ● ● ● ● ● ● ● ● ● ●

CHAPTER 10

A FEW LEGENDS IN HOCKEY

On this day in Sorts History January 26 1961 Wayne Douglas Gretzky was born in Brantford Ontario Canada
Gretzky played in the WHA for the Indianapolis Racers

He played in the NHL for the Edmonton Oiler —The Los Angeles Kings—The St. Louis Blues—The New York Rangers

Wayne Gretzky played 20 years in the NHL, he retired in 1999

Highlights of Wayne Gretzky's career

Many Sportswriters consider Wayne Gretzky as the greatest Hockey Player of all time, Gretzky is also known as "The Great One" by The League, The Players, The Fans, and like I said, most Sportswriters

Wayne Gretzky is the Leading Scorer in NHL history.

Wayne Gretzky has more goals and assists than any other player that has ever played in the NHL!

He had more assists than any other player towards total points and he is the only player to total over 200 points in a single season, a feat he accomplished on four different occasions. .

Wayne Gretzky tallied over 100 points in 16 professional seasons, he had 14 of the 16 in consecutive seasons. When he retired in 1999 Gretzky had a grand total of 61 NHL Records.

Gretzky had 40 regular season records, 15 Playoff Records, and 6 All Star Records,

As of 2015 Wayne Gretzky still held 60 of the 61 records he established before he retired in 1999

Gretzky Led the Edmonton Oilers to 4 Stanley Cup Championships, A couple of Months after their last Stanley Cup win on August 9 1988 The Oilers traded Gretzky to the L.A. Kings

Wayne Gretzky is credited for popularizing Hockey in California and most likely some other States.

In his careen Wayne Gretzky won 9 Hart Trophies as the Most Valuable Player

He won 10 Hart Trophies for most points in a season. He won 2 Conn Smythe Trophies as playoff Most Valuable Player

Wayne Gretzky won 5 Lester B. Pearson Awards which is now called The Ted Lindsay Award, for Most Outstanding Player as Judged by his Peers

Gretzky won The Lady Byng Trophy5 times for Sportsmanship and Performance.

Wayne Douglas Gretzky was inducted into the NHL Hall of Fame in 1999

On this day in Sports History august 4 1921 Joseph Henri Maurice Richard was born in Montreal Quebec

On this day in Sports History Maurice Richard passed away on May 27, 2000 Maurice 'The Rocket" Richard was a national hero and he was the first Canadian Athlete to be honored With a State Funeral.

Maurice Richard was revered by the Francophone Community, and he well deserved it, He was a hero and a Legend at the same time.

Highlights of Maurice Richard's Hockey career

Maurice Richard earned the nickname The "Rocket" because of his amazing speed on the ice.

Richard scored his first of many goals in the NHL on November 8 1942 Against the New York Ranger

Richard retired with 544 goals in a great Hockey career.

In the 1944-45 season Richard was the first player in the NHL to score 50 goals in a season He accomplished this feat in 50 games.

In 1947 Maurice Richard won The Hart Trophy as the NHL's Most Valuable Player

Maurice Richard led his Montreal Canadian team mates to 8 Stanley Cup Titles in his 18 year NFL career

Five of the 8 Stanley Cup Wins were in succession which is a NHL record

Richard and The Canadians won the Stanley Cups—5 times in a Row 1956—1957—1958—1959—1960

Up until the 1943-44 season, Richard wore jersey number 15, but the birth of His daughter Huguette, who weighed 9 Pounds at birth he changed fro 15 to 9 to match her weight at birth.

The Canadians retired The Rockets Number 9 in 1960.

The Canadians donated The Maurice "Rocket" Richard Trophy to the National Hockey League, the award is given every year to the player that leads the league in scoring..

Richard was the first player in the NHL to score 500 career goals.

Richard was selected to The First Team All Star team—8 times——1944-45—4546—46-47—4748—4849—49-50—50-51—51-52

Maurice Richard was selected to The Second Team —6 times———

!943-44—50-51—51-52—52-53—53-54—56-57— **For a total of 14 All Star Games**

In 2017 Richard was named one of the top 100 greatest players in NHL History

The Canadian Press Named Maurice Richard The Male Athlete of The Year—3 times—1952—1957—1958

In 1975 he was inducted into Canada Sports Hall of Fame

Joseph Henri Maurice Richard was inducted into The NHL Hall of Fame in 1961

⚬⚬⚬⚬⚬

On this day in Sports History March 20, 1948 Robert Gordon Orr was born in Parry Sound Ontario, Canada

Robert Gordon Orr, AAK Bobby Orr went on to be one of the greatest Hockey players of all time.

Orr played in the NHL for 10 seasons with the Boston Bruins. Bobby Orr played his last two seasons in the NHL for the Chicago Blackhawks

Highlights Of Bobby Orr's NHL career

In 1966 Orr joined the Boston Bruins at the age of 18, The Boston Bruins had not won a Stanley Cup since 1941. And did not qualify for the play-off's since 1969; with Bobby Orr the Boston Bruins won The Stanley Cup—2 times —1970—1972 —In the final game Orr scored the winning goal in both Games

Orr was named the Play-off's Most Valuable Player—2 times 1970—1972—

Bobby Orr is the only defenseman to win the scoring title —2 times—1970—1972

Orr won the Norris Trophy in consecutive years —8 times—1967-68 —1968-69—1969-70—1970-71—1971-72—1972-73—1973—74 1974-75

Bobby Orr won the Calder Memorial Trophy—1966-67- season.

He won the Art Ross Trophy—1969-70- season.

Orr won the Hart Memorial Trophy—1969-70-season

Orr won the Conn Smythe Trophy —1969-70-season

Bobby Orr won the Hart Memorial Trophy—1971-72- season

Orr won the Conn Smythe Trophy— 1971-72-season

Orr won the Art Ross Trophy—1974-75

Bobby Orr won the Lester B. Pearson Award —1974-75

Orr was named one of the 100 greatest NHL players in history during An All Star Ceremony in Los Angeles on January 17, 2017

Bobby Orr was inducted into the Hall of Fame; at the Age of 31 he was the youngest player to ever have been inducted

Robert Gordon Orr was inducted into the NHL Hockey Hall of Fame in 1979

● ● ● ● ● ● ● ● ● ● ● ● ● ● ● ● ● ●

CHAPTER 11

ON THIS DAY IN SPORTS HISTORY BOXING

On this day in Sports History August 31,1969 Rocky Marciano died in a plane crash near Newton Iowa..Marciano was ranked by boxing historians as one of the greatest boxers of all time. He retired from boxing undefeated with a perfect 49 wins and no losses. Of the 49 wins, 43 were by knock-outs. He won the title in 1952 by KO over Jersey Joe Walcott

On this day in Sports History October 28, 2006Trevor Berbick, who once defeated Muhammad Ali, Berbick was only 52 when he was Killed, in Jamaika. His nephew and another nut were later convicted.

On this day in Sports History, July 8 1976 Sugar ray Leonard won the Gold Medal for the United States in the Summer Olympics. Leonard won all five of his Light Welterweight matches 5-0.

On this day in Sports History, December, 16, 1918, Jack Dempsey KO'S Carl Morris in 14 seconds of the firs round.

On this day in Sports History October 29,1960CassiusClay, (Muhammad Ali) won his first fight, He won a six rounder against Tunney Hunsaker. From that point on to the end of 1963 he amassed a record of 19 wins and no losses with 15 of the wins were by knock-outs

On this day in Sports History, March 13, 1963 Ali had one of the toughest fights of his career, his opponent; Doug Jones lost a unanimous decision, and the crowd booed and debris was thrown into the ring in anger.

On this day in Sports History; February 25, 1964 Cassius Clay won the heavyweight championship by defeating Sonny Liston in Miami Beach, Florida. Cassius Clay later changed his name to Muhammad Ali

On this day in Sports History; October 1, 1975 Joe Frasier and Muhammad Ali squared off for the Heavyweight Championship of the world The fight was held in the Philippines, prior to the fight Muhammad Ali did some heavy taunting to Joe Frasier, which set he stage for one of the Greatest fights of all time. Joe Frasier's Manager threw in the towel at the end of the 14th round, which gave Ali the win by TKO. Ali later claimed it was one of the toughest fights he ever had.

In 2005 Muhammad Ali was awarded the Presidential Medal of Freedom which is the highest honor given to a US citizen by the President in office. President George W Bush made the presentation

On this day in Sports History August 17, 1987 Muhammad Ali was inducted into The Boxing Hall of Fame

On this day in Sports History; On April 29, 1967 Muhammad Ali was stripped of his Heavyweight title because he refused to be inducted into the US Army. Ali refused induction on religious grounds.

On this day in Sports History; October 30 in Zaire, (The Rumble in the Jungle) Muhammad Ali KO'S George Forman in the 8th round

On this day in Sports History November 25, 1980 Sugar Ray Leonard Was awarded the Welterweight Championship after Roberto Duran quit the fight in the 8th round of their Championship fight

On this day in Sports History November 22, 1986; Mike Tyson defeated the Champion Trevor Berbick in2:35 of the second round to win the undisputed heavyweight Championship of the world.

On this day in Sports History; November 8, 1985 Rubin "hurricane" Carter was released from prison after serving nearly 20 years for a triple homicide in 1966. Public pressure and the help from celebrities such as Bob Dylan and others who supported Carter, Eventually A New Jersey district judge overturned the conviction, citing racism and mistakes by the prosecution.

On this day in Sports History September 1926 Jack Dempsey lost his title by decision to Gene Tunney

CWMO

●　●　●　●　●　●　●　●　●　●　●　●　●　●　●　●　●

CHAPTER 12

A FEW LEGENDS IN BOXING

On this day in Sports History September 1 1923 Rocco Francis Marchegiano, aka Rocky Marciano was born in Brockton Massachusetts

On this day in Sports History August 31 one day before his 46th birthday Rocky was a passenger a small private plane that crashed. It was a night, the plane hit a tree about 2 miles short of the runway. The pilot Glen Belz hat 231 hours of flying time, 35 of them were at night. He had no instrument rating. Belz was trying to land the plane on a small airfield outside Newton Iowa. Lew Farrel a former Boxer who was childhood friend of Rocky Marciano ; his son, Frankie Farell was killed along with betz and Marciano.

Highlights of Rocky Marciano's Boxing Career

Marciano boxed as a professional from 1947 to 195 5 He was the Heavyweight Champion from 1952 till 1956. Rocky Marciano was the only Heavyweight Champion to retire from the ring **undefeated As a professional fighter. His record was—49 fights —49 wins!!!**

He had six title defenses First against Jersey Joe Walcott on May 15, 1953 —Marciano won the fight by knockout in the first round. The fight was held in Chicago

On September 24, in 1953 Marciano beat Roland LaStarza with a KO in the 11th round, the fight was held in New York .

On June 19th 1954 Marciano won by decision over Ezzard Charles in 15 rounds- The fight was held in New York

On September 17th 1954 In a rematch against Ezzard Charles Marciano won with a knockout in the 8th round. The fight was held in New YOrk

On May 16th 1955In San Francisco Rocky Marciano won by knockout over Don Cockell in the 9th round.

On September 21 1955,he defeated Archie Moore with a knockout in the 9th round The fight was held in New York

As it turned out this would be Rocky Marciano's last fight.

Of the first 25 professional fights Marciano won the all by knockout except for 2 of them As a Matter of fact; of the 49 wins in his career 43 were by knockouts only six were by decision. Ezzard Charles was the only boxer to last 15 rounds with Rocky Marciano..

The following is a list of Marciano's 49 wins and no losses.

On may17, 1947 Lee Epperson KO in the first Rocky Marciano's first of 49 Professional Fight

1948=10 fights

On July 12, 1948 John Edwards KO in the first
On April 9,1 948 Bobby Quinn KO in 3
On August 23 1948 Eddie Ross KO in the first
On August 30 1948 Jimmy Weeks KO in the first
On September 13 1948 Jerry Jackson KO in the first
On September 20 1948 Bill Hardeman KO in the first
On September 30 1948 Gil Cardione KO in the first
On October 4 1948 Bob Jefferson KO in the 2nd round

ON November 29 1948 Patrick Jefferson KO in he first

On December 14 1948 Gilley Ferron KO in the 2nd round

1949= 13 fights

On March 21 1949 Johnny Pretzie KO in round 5

On March28 1949 Artie Donator KO in first

On April11 1949 James Walls KO in round 3

On May 2 1949 Jimmy Evans KO in round 3

On May 23 1949 Don Mogard Decision 10 rounds

On July 18 1949 Harry Haft KO in round 3

On August 16 1949 Pete Louthis KO in round 3

On September 26 1949 Tommy Giorgio KO in round 4

On October 10 1949 Ted Lowry Decision 10 rounds

On November 7 1949 Joe Domonic KO in round 2

On December 2 1949 Pat Richards KO in round 2

On December 19 1949 Phil Muscato KO in round 5

On December 30 1949 Carmine Vingo KO in round 6

1950=6 fights

On March 24 1950 Roland LaStarza Decision 10 rounds

On June 5 1950 Eldridge Eatman KO in round 3

On July10 1950 Gino Buonvino KO in round 10

On September 18 1950 Johnny Shkor KO in round 6

On November 13 1950 Ted Lowry Decision 10 rounds

On December 18 1950 Bill Wilson KO in first round

1951= 7 fights

On January 29 1951 Keene Simmons KO in round 8

On March 20 1951 Harold Mitchell KO in round 2

On March 26 1951 Art Henri KO in round 9

On April 30 1951 Red Applegae Decision 10 rounds

On July 12 1951 Rex Layne KO in round 6

On August 27 195 Freddie Beshore KO in round 4

On October 26 1951 Joe Louis KO in round 8

1952=5 fights

On February 13 1952 Lee Savold KO in round 6
On April 21 1952 Gino Buonvino KO in round 2
On may 12 1952 Bernie Reynolds KO in round 3
On July 28 1952 Harry Mathews KO in round 2

On September 23 1952 Marciano won over Jersey Joe Walcott for the Heavyweight Championship of the world He won with a KO in the in round 13

1953=2 fights

On may 151953 Jersey Joe Walcott KO in the first
On September 24 1953 Roland LaStarza KO in round 11

1954=2 fights

On June 19 1954 Ezzard Charles; Marciano wins by decision 15 rounds
On September17 1954 Ezzard Charles KO in round 8·

!955=2 fights

On May 16 1955 Don Cockell KO in round 9·
On September 21 1955 Archie Moore KO in round 9

Ring Magazine was established in 1922. The Magazine has been naming the fighter of the Year since 1928 Rocky Marciano was named by ring the fighter of the year 3 times, First in 1952, then in 1954 and again in 1055

On this day In Sports History April 27 1956 Rocky Marciano Announced His retirement from Boxing

Rocky Marciano was inducted into the International Boxing Hall of Fame in 1990

Marciano was also inducted into the World Boxing Hall of Fame

On this day in Sports History June 24 1895 William Harrison "jack" Dempsey was born, Nicknamed "Kid Blackie" and "The Manassa Mauler."

On this day in Sports History May 1 1983 the Boxing World lost, one of the Greatest Heavyweight Fighters of all time: The great Jack Dempsey died in New York City

Highlights of Jack Dempsey's Career

Dempsey competed in the ring from 1914 until 1927; He became the Heavyweight Champion in 1919 and held the title till 1927. Jack Dempsey became one of the most popular fighters in boxing history

Jack Dempsey Had a total of 75 fights, his record was 54 wins (44 by KO) 6 losses and 9 draws.

Dempsey quit school to work and help the family financially and later left home at age 16.

Later in life, as the Heavyweight Champion his title defending fights His endorsements and the movies made Jack Dempsey a very rich man.

Jack Dempsey may have been racially motivated because after winning the title he said he would no longer fight black boxers.

In 1924 Dempsey became an executive in the Irish Workers League: the Irish Workers League was founded by Irish Labor leader Jim Larkin. The I.W.L. was a Soviet-backed Communist group that was founded in Dublin Ireland. What was odd is that Jack Dempsey lost his title to Gene Tunney who was an Irish American and a former U.S. Marine.

On July 4 1919 Jack Dempsey Defeated Jess Willard in Toledo Ohio for the Heavyweight Championship of the World. Willard Was known as the "Pottawatamie Giant" he was 6'61/2 inches tall and weighed 245 pounds, While Dempsey was 6' 1" and 187 pounds.

Dempsey knocked Willard down seven times in the first round

After Dempsey won the title he had 8 more fights, He had 67 fights up to that point which he won 39 of them by knockouts

On September 6, 1919 in fight number 68 Of his career Dempsey won by KO in 1.13 seconds of the 3rd round He beat Billy Miske in his first defense of his title. The fight was held in the Floyd Fitzsimmons Arena in Benton Harbor Michigan

On December 14, 1920 in fight number 69 Dempsey won by KO in 1.57 seconds of the 12th round. He beat Bill Branan in his second defense of his title. The fight was held at Madison Square Gardens,in New York City, New York

On July 2, 1921 In fight number 70 Dempsey won by KO over George Carpentier in the 4th round. The fight was held at Boyles Thirty Acres in Jersey City, New Jersey he won the Vacant NBA Title and retained his Heavyweight Title

On July 4 1923 in fight number 71, Dempsey Defeated Tommy Gibbons by Decision in 15 rounds. The fight was held in Shelby Montana. Jack Dempsey retained The Ring and his Heavyweight Title

On September 14, 1923 In fight number 72 Dempsey won by KO in 0.57 seconds of round 2 over Lois Angel Firpo.The fight was held in New York City New York. Jack Dempsey retained the NYSAC, The Ring and the World Heavyweight Title

On September 23, 1926 in fight number 73 of his career Jack Dempsey Lost by unanimous decision to Gene Tunney. The fight was held at Sesquicentennial Stadium in Philadelphia Pennsylvania Jack Dempsey lost The NBA Title, the Ring, and the Heavyweight Title of he Worl

On September 22, 1927 Gene Tunney won a Unanimous decision over Jack Dempsey to retain his NBA Title the Ring, and the Heavyweight Title of the World. The fight was held at Soldiers Field in Chicago Illinois

On this day in Sports History May 13, 1914 Joseph Louis Barrow was born in Lafayette Alabama. He was better known as Joe Louis, He was also known by his nickname "The Brown Bomber."

On this day in Sports History April 12, 1981 Joe Louis died in Paradise Nevada, He was 66 when he passed away.

Highlights of Joe Louis's career in boxing

Joe Louis was one of my favorite athletes of all-time, what a great Champion he was. (His love for golf might have had a little bit to do with my opinion of Louis.)

In Riverdale Illinois "The Champ" Golf Course was named in his honor. In 1952, Louis was helpful in breaking the sports color barrier in the U. S. by appearing under a sponsor's exemption in a PGA even.

In 1926 A gang of white men in the Ku Klux Klan had a profound effect on Louis's family, and the family moved to Detroit Michigan.

Joe Louis Started his professional career in boxing in 1934 and competed in the ring till 1951.

He had a total of 69 fights; he won 66 of them, (52 by KO) and he had 3 losses

He held he Heavyweight Championship from 1937 to 1949

In 2005 The International Boxing Research Organization ranked Joe Louis as the greatest fighter of all time.

Joe Louis was also ranked number one by Ring Magazine as the greatest Puncher of all time.

Joe Louis had 26 Championship fights. The only fighter with more is Julio Cesar Chavez who had 27 title fights

In his 33rd fight on June 22, 1937 Joe Louis defeated James J. Braddock by KO in round 8. The fight was held at, Comiskey Park, Chicago Illinois, He won the NBA, NYSAC The Ring, and World Heavyweight Titles.

He following is a list of the 26 title fights Joe Louis had.

On August 30, 1937, Against Tommy Farr, he won by unanimous decision, 15 rounds. The fight was held in Yankee Stadium, New York City, New York. Louis retained The Ring and Heavyweight titles.

On February 23, 1938, Against Nathan Mann, he won by KO in 1:36 seconds of the round 3. The fight was held in Madison Square Garden New York City, New York. He retained The Ring, and World Heavyweight itles

ON April 4, 1938 Against Harry Thomas, he won by KO in 2:50 seconds of round 5. The fight was held at Chicago Stadium, Chicago Illinois. He retained The Ring and World Heavyweight titles.

On June 22 1938 Against Max Schmeling, he won by KO in 2:04 seconds of round 1. The fight was held at Yankee Stadium, New York City, New York. Louis retained The NBA, NYSAC, The Ring and World Heavyweight titles.

On January 25, 1939 Against John Henry Lewis, he won by KO in 2:29 seconds of round 1. The fight was held at Madison Square Garden, New York City, New York. He retained The Ring and World Heavyweight titles

On April 17, 1939 Against Jack Roper, Joe Louis won by KO in 2:20 seconds of round 1. The fight was held in Los Angeles California, Louis retained The Ring and the World Heavyweight Titles.

On June 28, !939 Against Tony Galento, Louis won by TKO in 2:29 seconds of round 5. The fight was held at Yankee Stadium, New York City, New York. He retained The Ring, and World Heavyweight Titles.

On September 20, 1939, Against Bob Pastor, Louis won by KO in 0:38 seconds of round 11. The fight was held at Briggs Stadium, Detroit Michigan. He retained The Ring and World Heavyweight Titles.

On February 9, 1940 Against Arturo Godoy, Louis won by split decision he fight went 15 rounds. The fight was held at Madison Square Garden, New York City, New York. He retained The Ring and the World Heavyweight titles.

On March 29, 1940, Against Johnny Paychek, Louis won by TKO in 0:41seconds of round 2. The fight was held at Madison Square Garden, New York City, New York. He retained The Ring and the World Heavyweight Titles.

ON June 20, 1940 Against Arturo Godoy, he won by TKO in 1:24 seconds of round 8. The fight was held at Yankee Stadium, New York City, New York. He retained The Ring and the World Heavyweight Titles.

On December 16, 1940 Against Al McCoy Louis won by RTD of round 5. The fight was held at Boston Garden in Boston Massachusetts. Joe Louis retained The Ring and World Heavyweight Titles.

On January 31, 1941 Against Red Berman, he won by KO in 2:49 seconds of round 5. The fight was held at Madison Square Garden, New York City, New York. He retained The Ring and World Heavyweight titles.

On February 17, 1941 Against Gus Dorazio he won by KO in 1:30 Seconds of round 2. The fight was held at Convention Hall, Philadelphia Pennsylvania. He retained The Ring and the World Heavyweight titles.

On March 31, 1941 Against Abe Simon, he won by TKO in 1:20 of round 13. The fight was held in Detroit Michigan. He retained The Ring and World Heavyweight titles.

On May 23, 1941 Against Buddy Baer he won by Disqualification in 3 minutes of round 7. The fight was held at Griffith Stadium, Washington D. C. He retained The Ring and Heavyweight titles. Buddy Baer was disqualified after his Manager refused to leave the ring.

On June 18, 1941 against Billy Conn he won by KO in 2:58 round 13. The fight was held at the Polo Grounds New York City New York. He retained The Ring and World Heavyweight titles

On August 4, 194i against Tony Musto he won by TKO in 1:36 of round 9. The fight was held at the St Louis Arena, St Louis Missouri. He retained The Ring and World Heavyweight titles.

On September 29, 1941 against Lou Nova he won by TKO in 2:59 of round 6. The fight was held at the Polo Grounds, New York City, New York. He retained The Ring and World Heavyweight titles.

On January 9, 1942, against Buddy Baer, he won by KO in 2:56 second of round 1. The fight was held at Madison Square Garden, New York City, New York. He retained The Ring and World Heavyweight titles.

On March 27, 1942 against Abe Simon, he won by TKO in 16 seconds of round 6. The fight was held at Madison Square Garden, New York City, New York. He retained the Ring and World Heavyweight titles.

On November 14, 1944 against Johnny Davis he won by TKO in 53 seconds of round 1. The fight was held in the Memorial Auditorium, Buffalo New York He retained NYSAC, and Heavyweight title.

On June 19, 1946 against Billy Conn he won by KO in 2;19 seconds of round 8. The fight was held at Yankee Stadium, New York City, New York. He retained The Ring and World Heavyweight titles.

On September 18, 1946 against Tami Mauriello he won by KO in 2;09 seconds of round 1. The fight was held at Yankee Stadium, New York City New York. He retained The Ring and World Heavyweight titles.

On December 5, 1947, against Jersey Joe Walcott he won by split decision (15 rounds) The fight was held At Madison Square Garden, New York City, New York. He retained The Ring and World Heavyweight titles

On June 25, 1948, against Jersey Joe Walcott, he won by KO in Round 11. The fight was held at Yankee Stadium, New York City, New York. He retained The Ring and World Heavyweight titles.

On September 27, 1950, against Ezzard Charles, Joe Louis lost The Ring and the Heavyweight Championship of the World. He lost the fight by unanimous decision in 15 rounds. The fight was held at Yankee Stadium, New York City, New York.

On this day in Sports History, January 17, 1942 Cassius Clay Jr. was born in Louisville Kentucky. Cassius Clay later changed his name to Muhammad Ali. Ali was also know as; "The Greatest", "The Louisville Lip", "The peoples Champion" and he called himself "The King of Boxing", Ali was not a very shy individual. When he changed his name from Cassius Clay which he said was his slave name To Muhammad Ali he was in hopes of setting an example of racial pride for African Americans.

On this day in Sports History, June 3, 2016, the boxing world lost a great Champion, Muhammad Ali died in Scottsdale Arizona at the age of 74.

It was not only the boxing world that lost a great Champion, but the entire Sports World lost a great Champion. We lost the guy that could "float like a Butterfly and sting like a Bee."

Highlights of Muhammad Ali's career in boxing

Muhammad Ali had 61 bouts, his record is 56 wins and 5 losses, 37 of his wins were by knockouts and 19 were by decision. Ali lost 4 fights by decision and he lost 1 fight by KO. Muhammad Ali won the heavyweight title when he was 22 years and 39 days old, and he lost his last fight to Trevor Berbick when he was 39 years and 328 days old.

On February 25, 1964 against Sonny Liston he won by RTD in 3:00 of round 6. The fight was held at the Convention Center in Miami Beach Florida, he won the WBC, the Ring and Lineal Heavyweight Titles.

On May 25, 1965, against Sonny Liston he won by KO in 2:12 seconds of round 1. The fight was held at The Civic Center in Lewiston Maine. He retained The WBC, the Ring and Lineal Heavyweight Titles.

On November 22, 1965, against Floyd Patterson, he won by TKO in 2:18 seconds of round 12. The fight was held at the Las Vegas Convention Center, in Winchester Nevada. He retained WBC, the Ring and Lineal Heavyweight Titles.

ON March 29, 1966, against George Chuvalo, he won by unanimous decision, in 15 rounds. The fight was held at The Maple Leaf Garden, in Toronto Canada. He retained The WBC, the Ring, and Lineal Heavyweight Titles.

On May 21, 1966, against Henry Cooper, he won by TKO in !:38 seconds of round 6. The fight was held in Arsenal Stadium, In London England. He retained the WBC, the Ring and Lineal Heavyweight Titles.

On August 6, 1966, against Brian London, he won by KO in 1:40 seconds of round 3. The fight was held at Earls Court Exhibition Center, London England. He retained the WBC, the Ring and Lineal Heavyweight Titles.

On September 10, 1966, against Karl Mildenberger, he won by TKO in 1:30 seconds of round 12. The fight was held at Waldstadion in Frankfurt

West Germany. He retained the WBC the Ring and Lineal Heavyweight Titles.

On November 14, 1966, against Cleveland Williams, he won by TKO in !:08 seconds of round 3. The fight was held in the Astrodome in Houston Texas. He retained the WBC the Ring and Lineal Heavyweight Titles.

On February 6, 1967, against Ernie Terrell, he won by unanimous decision in 15 rounds. The fight was held at the Astrodome in Houston Texas. He won the WBA, and he retained the WBC, the Ring and Lineal Heavyweight Titles.

ON March 22, 1967, against Zora Folley, he won by KO in 1;48 seconds of round 7. The fight was held at Madison Square Garden in New York City, New York, he retained the WBA, WBC the Ring and Lineal Heavyweight Titles.

On October 26, 1970, against Jerry Quarry, he won by RTD in 3 minutes of round 3. The fight was held at the Municipal Auditorium in Atlanta Georgia, he retained the WBA, WBC, the Ring and Lineal Heavyweight Titles.

On December 7, 1970, against Oscar Bonavena, he won by TKO in 2:03 seconds of round 15. The fight was held at Madison Square Garden in New York City, New York he retained the WBA, WBC, the Ring and Lineal Heavyweight Titles.

ON March8, 1971, against Joe Frazier, he lost by unanimous decision in 15 rounds. The fight was held at Madison Square Garden, in New York City, New York. He lost the WBA, WBC, the Ring, and Lineal Heavyweight Titles.

On July 26, 1971, against Jimmy Ellis, he won by TKO in 2:10 seconds of round 12. The fight was held at the Astrodome in Houston Texas, he won the vacant NABF Heavyweight Title.

On November 17, 1971, against Buster Mathis, he won by UD, the fight went 12 rounds. The fight was held at the Astrodome, in Houston Texas, he retained the NABF Heavyweight Title.

On December 26, 1971, against Jurgen Blin, he won by KO in 2:12 seconds of round 7. The fight was held at Hallenstadion, in Zurich Switzerland, he retained the NABF Heavyweight Title.

On April 1, 1972, against Mac Foster, he won by unanimous decision in 15 rounds. The fight was held at Nippon Budokan, Tokyo Japan, he retained the NABF Heavyweight Title

On May 1, 1972, against George Chuvalo, he won by unanimous decision in 12 rounds. The fight was held at the Pacific Coliseum, in Vancouver British Columbia, Canada, he retained the NABF Heavyweight Title.

On June 27, 1972, against Jerry Quarry, he won by TKO in 19 seconds of round 7. The fight was held at the Las Vegas Convention Center, in Winchester Nevada, he retained the NABF.

On July19, 1972, against Alvin Lewis, he won by TKO in 1:15 seconds of round 11. The fight was held at Croke Park, in Dublin Ireland, he retained the NABF Heavyweight Title

On September 20, 1972, against Floyd Patterson, he won by RTD In 3 minutes of round 7. The fight was held at Madison Square Garden, in New York City, New York, he retained the NABF Heavyweight Title.

On November 21, 1972, against Bob Foster, he won by KO in 40 seconds of round 8. The fight was held at the Sahara Tahoe, at Stateline Nevada, he retained the NABF Heavyweight Title.

On February 14, 1973, against Joe Bugner, he won by unanimous decision in 12 rounds. The fight was held at the Las Vegas Convention Center in Winchester Nevada, he retained the NABF Heavyweight Title.

On March 31, 1973, against Ken Norton, he lost by split decision in 12 rounds. The fight was held at the Sports Arena in San Diego, California Ali lost the NABF Heavyweight Title.

On September 10, 1973, against Ken Norton, he won by split decision in 12 rounds. The fight was held at the Forum in Inglewood California, he won the NABF Heavyweight Title.

On October 20, 1973, against Rudie Lubbbers, he won by unanimous decision in 12 rounds. The fight was held at Gelora Bung Karno Stadium, in Jakarta, Indonesia, he retained the NABF Heavyweight Title.

On January 28, 1974, against Joe Frazier, he won by unanimous decision in 12 rounds. The fight was held at Madison Square Garden, in New York City, New York, he retained the NABF heavyweight Title.

On October 30, 1974, against George Foreman, he won by KO in 2:58 seconds of round 8. The fight was held at Stade Du 20 Mai in Kinshasa Zaire, he won the WBA, WBC, the Ring and Lineal Heavyweight Titles

On March 24, 1975, against Chuck Wepner, he won by TKO in 2:41 seconds of round 15. The fight was held at the Caliseum, in Richfield Ohio, he retained the WBA, WBC, the Ring and Lineal Heavyweight Titles.

On May 16, 1975, against Ron Lyle he won by TKO in 1:08 seconds of round 11. The fight was held at the Las Vegas Convention Center, in Winchester Nevada, he retained the WBA, WBC, the Ring and Lineal Heavyweight Titles.

On June 30, 1975, against Joe Bugner, he won by unanimous decision, the fight went 15 rounds, The fight was held at Stadium Merdeka, in Kuala Lumpur, Malaysia, he retained the WBA, WBC, the Ring and Lineal Heavyweight Titles.

On October 1, 1975, against Joe Frazier, he won by TKO in 3 minutes of round 14. The fight was held at the Philippine Coliseum in Quezon

City, Philippines, he retained the WBA, WBC, the Ring and Lineal Heavyweight Titles.

On February 20, 1976, against Jean-Pierre Coopman, he won by KO in 2:46 seconds of round 5. The fight was held at the Roberto Clemente Coliseum, in San Juan Puerto Rico, he retained the WBA, WBC, the Ring and Lineal Heavyweight Titles.

On April 30, 1976, against Jimmy Young, he won by unanimous decision in 15 rounds. The fight was held at the Capital Centre, in Landover, Maryland, he retained the WBA, the WBC, the Ring and Lineal Heavyweight Titles.

On May 24, 1976, against Richard Dunn, he won by TKO in 2:05 seconds of round 5. The fight was held at Olympiahalle, in Munich West Germany, he retained the WBA, the WBC, the Ring, and Lineal Heavyweight Titles.

On September 28, 1976, against Ken Norton, he won by unanimous decision in 15 rounds. The fight was held at Yankee Stadium, in New York City New York, he retained the WBA, the WBC, the Ring and Lineal Heavyweight Titles.

On May 16, 1977, against Alfredo Evangelista, he won by unanimous decision in 15 rounds. The fight was held at Capital Centre in Landover Maryland, he retained the WBA, the WBC, the Ring and Lineal Heavyweight Titles.

On September 29, 1977, against Ernie Shavers, he won by unanimous decision in 15 rounds. The fight was held at Madison Square Garden, in New York City, New York, he retained the WBA, the WBC, the Ring and Lineal heavyweight Titles.

On February 15, 1978, against Leon Spinks, he lost by split decision in 15 rounds. The fight was held at the Las Vegas Hilton, in Winchester Nevada, Ali lost the WBA, WBC, the Ring and Lineal Heavyweight Titles.

Ray G. Claveran

On September 15, 1978, against Leon Spinks, Ali won by unanimous decision in 15 rounds. The fight was held at the Superdome in New Orleans, Louisiana. Muhammad Ali won the WBA, the WBC, the Ring and Lineal Heavyweight Titles

On October 2, 1980, against Larry Holmes, Ali lost by RTD in 3 minutes of round 10. The fight was held Caesars Palace in Paradise, Nevada The fight was for the WBC, vacant Ring, and Lineal Heavyweight Titles

On December 11, 1981, against Trevor Berbick, Ali lost by unanimous decision in 10 rounds. The fight was held at the Queen Elizabeth Sports Centre, in Nassau, Bahamas

On August17, 1987, Muhammad Ali was inducted into The Boxing Hall of Fame

CHAPTER 13

ON THIS DAY IN SPORTS HISTORY OLYMPIC TRACK

MEN

On this day in Sports History August 9, 1936, In Berlin Germany, with Adolph Hitler in attendance; Jesse Owens won his 4th Gold Medal In the 4 X 100 meter sprint. He set the Worlds Record in the, !00 meter that stood for 20 year, and the Long Jump Record Lasted for 25 years.

On this day In sports History, October 28, 1949, Bruce Jenner was born. In 1976 At the Olympics in Montreal Canada he won the gold medal, he set the world record with a score of 8,614 points. In 2015 Bruce legally changed his name to Caitlyn and became a woman.

On this day In Sports History, September 24, 1988, at the Seoul Olympics Ben Johnson of Canada won the Gold Medal, and set a New Worlds Record in the 100 Meter race. Ben Johnson was stripped of his Gold Medal after he tested positive for a banned substance.

On this day in Sports History, October 12, 1983, the Olympic Committee Reinstated the 2 Gold Medals that Jim Thorpe won in the 1912 Olympics held in Stockholm Sweden, Jim Thorpe was stripped of his medals because he played in a semi Professional baseball game before competing in the Stockholm Olympics. The medals were returned to his family in a ceremony that was held in Los Angeles California. Jim Thorpe was a member of the Sauk and the Fox Nation.

On this day in Sports History, June 11, 1968, Bob Beamon broke The World Record in the long jump at the Olympics held in Mexico City. His record Jump of 27feet 6 and a half inches has lasted for over 50 years, In 1968; Bob Beamon won 22 of the 23 meets he competed in,

On this day in Sports History, August14, 2014, Wayde van Niekerk of RSA, set a new World Record in the 400 meter event in the time of 43.03 seconds at the Olympics in Rio de Janeiro Brazil

On this day in Sports History, August 9, 2012, David Redisha, of Kenya set a new World Record in the 800 meter event in the time of 1:40.91 at the Olympics in London England

On this day in Sports History August 11, 2012 The Jamaica 4x100 relay team set a new World Record in the time of 36.84 seconds at the Olympics in London England

OLYMPICS TRACK
WOMEN

On this day in Sports History, September 21, 1998 Florence Griffith Joyner was only 38 when she died in Mission Viejo, California. Florence Griffith was born in Los Angeles California on December 21 1959. Her Birth name was Florence Delorez Griffith.

On this day In Sports History, September 29, 1988, Florence Griffith Joyner of the United States set a new World Record in the 200 meter in the time of 21.34. at the Olympics in Seoul Korea

On this day in Sports History, August 12, 2016 Almaz Ayana of Etheopia set a new World Record in the 10,000 meter run in the time of 29:17.45 at the Olympics in Rio de Janeiro

On this day in Sports History, September 24, 1988, Jackie Joyner- kersee of the United States set a new World Record in the Heptathlon with 7,291 Points at the Olympics in Seoul Korea

On this day in Sports History, August 10, 2012 Tianna Madison, Allison Felix, Bianca Knight, and Carmelita Jeter of the United States set a new World Record in the 4x100 meter Relay in the time of 40.82 seconds at the2012 Olympics in London England

On this day in October 1, 1988, Tatyana Ledovskaya, Olga Nazarova, Mariya Pinigina, and Olga Bryzgina set a new World Record in the 4x 400 Meter Relay in the time of 3:15.17 seconds at the 1988 Olympics in Seoul Korea

OLYMPICS SWIMMING
MEN

On this day in Sports History, August 4, 2012, Sun Yang of China set a New World Record in the 1500 Meter Freestyle Swimming event in the time of 14: 31.02 at the 2012 London Olympics.

On this day in Sports History August 13, 2016 Ryan Murphy set a new World Record in the 100 meter Backstroke in the time of 51.85 seconds at the 2016 Olympics in Rio de Janeiro, Brazil

On this day in Sports History August 7, 2016, Adam Peaty of Great Britain set a new World Record in the 100 meter Breaststroke in the time of 57.13 seconds at the 2016 Olympics in Rio de Janeiro, Brazil.

On this day in Sports History August 10, 2008 Michael Phelps of the United States set a new World Record in the 400 meter Individual Medley in the time of 4:03.84 in the 2008 Olympics in Beijing, China

On this day in Sports History August 11, 2008 Michael Phelps, Garrett Weber Gale, Cullun Jones and Jason Lezak of the United States, set a new World Record in the 4x 100 Meter Freestyle Relay in the time of 3:08.20 in the 2008 Olympics in Beijing, China

OLYMPICS SWIMMING
WOMEN

On this day in Sports History, August 7,2016 Kathie Ledecky of the United States set a new World Record in the 400 Meter Freestyle in the time of 3:56.46 seconds at the 2016 Olympics in Rio de Janeiro

On this day in Sports History, August 12,2016 Kathie Ledecky of the United States set a new World Record in the 800 Meter Freestyle in the time of 8:04.79 seconds at the 2016 Olympics in Rio de Janeiro

On this day in Sports History August 3, 2012 Missy Franklin of the United States set a new World Record in the 200 Meter Backstroke in the time of 2:04.06 seconds at the 2012 Olympics in London England.

On this day in Sports History, August 7, 2016, Sarah Sjostrom of Sweden set a new World Record in the 100 Meter Butterfly in the time of 55.48 seconds at the 2016 Olympics in Rio de Janeiro

On this day in Sports History, August 6 2016, Katinka Hosszu of Hungary set a new World Record in the 400 Meter Individual Medley in the time of 4:26.36 seconds At the 2016 Olympics in Rio de Janeiro

● ● ● ● ● ● ● ● ● ● ● ● ● ● ● ● ● ● ●

CHAPTER 14

A FEW LEGENDS IN THE OLYMPICS

On this day in Sports History, June 30, 1985, Michael Fred Phelps was born in Baltimore Maryland. Phelps, also known as the Baltimore Bullet or the Flying Fish is a living legend he acquired as member of the United States National Olympic Swimming team.

It is hard to imagine that any individual can accomplish so much in his sport of choice. In International competition Such as the World Championships, the Pan Pacific Championships and the Olympics Michael Phelps has won a total of 82 Medals in these major competitions. He won 65 Gold Medals 14 Silver Medals and 3 Bronze. Now is this not hard to fathom?

When we talk about legends of the Olympics, Michael Phelps name has to enter into the conversation, Phelps is the most decorated athlete in the history of the Olympics with a total of 28 Olympics Medals; 23 Gold— 3 Silver—2 Bronze. (WHEW!!! I feel if I ever met Phelps I would have to bow)

Highlight of Michael Phelps career in swimming

Michael Phelps Olympic career started in the 2004 Olympics held in Athens Greece. In those Olympics Phelps won — 6 Gold — and 2 Bronze Medals for a total of 8.

In the next Olympics in 2008 Held in Beijing China, he set a new record by winning — 8 Gold Medals In a single Olympics, in doing so he broke the record of 7 first place finishes in a single Olympics held by another American Swimmer, Mark Spitz. Michael Phelps now has a total of 16 Medals in his first 2 Olympics

In the next Olympics the 2012 Olympics held in London England Phelps won— 4 Gold —2 Silver. Now in the 3 Olympics Phelps has won a total of 22 Olympic medals

In Michael Phelps last Olympics held in Rio de Janeiro, The Baltimore Bullet won — 5 Gold Medals —1 Silver, for a grand total of 28 Olympic medals, 23 Gold—3 Silver—2 Bronze. Hmmm!

The following is the Olympics and the events in which he won the 23 Gold medals;

The 2004 Olympics held in Athens Greece:

The100 m Butterfly- **Gold;** —200 m Butterfly - **Gold;** —200 m Medley-**Gold**—400m Medley-**Gold**—4x 200 m Freestyle-**Gold.** —

4x100 m Medley- **Gold—Phelps also won 2 Bronze Medals in these 2004 Olympics**

The 2008 Olympics held in Beijing China;

200 m Freestyle - **Gold**—100m Butterfly – **Gold**—200 m Butterfly – **Gold**—200 m Medley - **Gold**—400 m Medley- **Gold** —4x100 m Freestyle – **Gold**—4x200 m Freestyle – **Gold**—4x100 m Medley – **Gold**. (8 **Gold**, not bad eh?)

The 2012 Olympics held in London, England;

100 m Butterfly – **Gold**—200m Medley – **Gold**—4x200 m Freestyle Gold—4x100m Medley – **Gold**—200 m Butterfly- **Silver— Phelps won 1 more silver in these 2012 Olympics**

The 2016 Olympics held in Rio de Janeiro, Brazil

200 m Butterfly – **Gold**—200 m Medley – **Gold** —4x100 m Freestyle- **Gold**—4x200m Freestyle – **Gold**—4x100 m Medley- **Gold—Phelps also won a Silver Medal in these 2016 Olympics**

Because of his record breaking performance in major international competition Phelps earned The American Swimmer of the Year a record 11 times, and he was named The World Swimmer of the Year 8 times. Phelps was named the Sportsman of the Year by Sports Illustrated due to his success in the 2008 Olympic Games, Michael Phelps was also won the Swimmer of the Year Award presented by FINA. (There is much more but I am running out of room.)

On this day in Sports History, September 12, 1913 James Cleveland Owens was born in Oakville Alabama.

On this day in Sports History, which was a very sad day for me, Jesse Owens, as he was known died in Tucson Arizona on March 31, 1980, he was only 66years old. Owens was buried in the Oakwood Cemetery in Chicago Illinois

Jesse Owens was a heavy smoker, for 30-35 years he smoked a pack a day, he was hospitalized with lung cancer in 1979. Jesse Owen died of the disease in 1980 with his wife and family members at his bedside.

I have a theory why Jesse Owens became such a fast runner in track: he was the youngest of ten children, with 9 brothers and sisters you better be fast!! When Jesse Owens was 9 years old his family moved to Cleveland Ohio, at that time he was called J.C. When his teacher at the new school asked him his name he replied J C and because of his Southern accent the teacher thought he said Jesse; the name stuck and he was known as Jesse Owens from then on until he passed away in 1980.

To my way of thinking it was Jesse Owens that set the stage for Jackie Robinson in Major League Baseball—Earl Lloyd in NBA Basketball-- Kenny Washington in NFL football, and— Willie O'ree in NHL Hockey.

Each one of these athletes went down in Sports History for breaking the color barrier in each of their respective sport.

I definitely do not mean in any way to diminish the work of the great men that have worked so hard for their battle in the civil rights Movement. I just don't think that Jesse Owens has been given enough credit for his achievements, not only for his athletic accomplishments but for the advancements of his race. It is my belief; that whether you like or dislike anybody, you must give credit where credit is do!!!

In his time Jesse Owens was considered by most Knowledgeable sports writers and sports fans as the greatest Track and Field athlete in history.

In 1935 at the Big Ten track meet held in Ann Arbor Michigan, in the span of 45 minutes Jesse Owens set 3 World Records and tied another one. These have been called the greatest 45 minutes in Sports History.

In 1935 a year prior to the 1936 Olympics, Owens set a world record in the Long jump of 26 ft 8 inches; that was not broken for 25 years by fellow American Ralph Boston in 1960.

In the 36) Olympics he was not only t he most successful with the 4 Gold Medals, but as a black man he was credited with disproving Hitler's myth of Aryan supremacy. What must have hurt Owens is the fact that he was not invited to the White House to shake hands with the President of the United States.

While attending the 1960 Olympics in Rome, Adi Dassler; the founder of Adidas offered Owens the first sponsorship for a male African American Athlete. (As I was typing this bit of history I noticed that the name Adidas, are the first letters of Adi Dassler's first and last name, ADIDAS —(interesting)

To me Jesse Owens was more than a a great Track Star he was a great man; just stop and think what he had to endure as a black super star in a racially motivated country at that time.

Highlights of Jesse Owens Career in the Olympics

Unfortunately for us, the sports fan, Jesse Owens participated in only one Olympics: the 1936 Games held in Berlin Germany with Adolph Hitler in the Stands. Owens won 4 Gold Medals at these Olympic Games.

On August 3, Owens won the Gold Medal in the 100 Meter in the time of 10.3 seconds

On August 4, Jesse Owens won the Long Jump with a jump of 26 ft.5 **inches.**

On August 5, Owens won the 200 Meter Sprint with a time of 20.4 seconds.

On August 9, Owens won the 4x100 Relay with Team-mates Ralph Metcalf, Frank Wycoff, and Foy Draper.

The following is a list of Honors and Awards earned by Jesse Owens for his contributions to Athletics and for his Race and Country

In 1936 Associated Press Named Owens Male Athlete of the year

In the same year 1936 the German Olympic Committee donated 4 English Oak saplings; one for each Gold Medal Owens won In the Berlin Games,

In 1970 Jesse Owens was inducted into the Alabama Sports Hall of Fame.

In 1976 he was awarded the Presidential Medal of Freedom by President Gerald Ford.

In the Same year he was made part of the Olympic Order for his fight against racism at the 1936 Olympics in Berlin Germany.

In 1980 A new Asteroid was discovered and was named 6758 Jesseowens in honor of Jesse Owens.

In 1981 USA Track and Field created the Jesse Owens Award which is given to the country's top Track and Field Athlete every year

In 1983, Owens was part of the inaugural class that was selected into the U.S. Olympic Hall of Fame.

In 1984 a street near the Olympic Stadium in Berlin Germany was renamed Jesse-Owens Alee in honor of Owens. In the same year a secondary school in Berlin-Lichtenberg was named in his honor

In March28 1990 Jesse Owens was awarded the Congressional Gold Medal by President George H.W. Bush, The award was presented Posthumously.

In 1990 and again in 1998 U.S. Postage Stamps were issued by the United States postal service to honor Jesse Owens.

In 1996 at the same time that the Olympic torch came through the community, 60 years after the 1936 Olympics, the town were Jesse Owens was born, Oakville, Alabama, dedicated the Jesse Owens Memorial Park, and a Museum in his honor. The wall Street Journal covered the event and and reported that a Bronze Plaque at the park with the inscription written by Poet Charles Ghigna:

May the light shine forever--as a symbol of all who run—for the freedom of the sport—for the spirit of humanity—for the memory of Jesse Owens.

In 2001The Ohio State University dedicated Jesse Owens Memorial Stadium for track and field events. There is a sculpture honoring Jesse Owens that occupies a place of honor in the esplanade leading to the rotunda entrance to Ohio Stadium. Jesse Owens competed for the Ohio State Buckeyes on the track surrounding the Football field that existed prior to the 2001 expansion of Ohio Stadium. The campus also houses three recreational centers for students and staff named in his honor.

In 2002, Scholar Molefi Kete Asante listed Jesse Owens on his list of 100 greatest African Americans. In Cleveland, Ohio a statue of Owens in his Ohio State Track Suit was installed at Fort Huntington Park, west of the old courthouse.

Phoenix Arizona named the Jesse Owens Medical Plaza in his honor, as well as the Jesse Owens Parkway. Jesse Owens Park, in Tucson, Arizona is a center of local youth athletics there.

In 2009 World Athletic Championships in Berlin Germany, all members of the United States Track and Field Team wore badges with JO to commemorate Owens victories in the same stadium 73 years before.

In 2010 the Ohio Historical proposed that Jesse Owens as a finalist from a state wide vote for inclusion in Statuary Hall at the United States capitol

On November 15, 2015the city of Cleveland, Ohio renamed East Roadway, to Jesse Owens Way.

The Coliseum Commissioners honored Jesse Owens with a Los Angeles Coliseum "Court of Honor" Plaque for his contribution to sports in Los Angeles.

ESPN Ranked Jesse Owen as the greatest North American athlete in Track and field of the Twentieth Century. **The Olympics Hall of Fame was established in 1979 and the first class was inducted in 1983, Jesse Owen was inducted into the Hall of Fame with the first group**

On this day in Sports history December 21, 1959, Florence Delores Griffith was born, she is better known by her married name Florence Griffith Joyner. She is also known by her nickname Flo-Jo. Her place of birth is Los Angeles, California

On this day in Sports History Florence Griffith Joyner died In Mission Viejo, California; she was only 38 years old.

Joyner is considered by most Track and Field Experts and many sports writers as the fastest woman of all time. She attended California State University, Northridge, and UCLA where she participated on the Track and Field Team

In 1980 Florence Griffith-Joyner qualified for the U.S. Olympic Team in the !00 Meter race, but because of the US Boycott that year she did not get to run, Florence made he debut in the 1984 Olympics held in Los Angeles.

In 1987 in the World Championships held in Rome, Italy she won Gold in the 4x100 m relay, and she won the Silver Medal in the 200 Meter Race.

Highlights of Florence Griffith Joyner's Olympic career representing the United States

In the 1984 Olympics held in Los Angeles Florence Griffith Joyner won the Silver Medal in the200 meter run.

In the 1988 Olympics held in Seoul Florence Griffith Joyner won Gold in the 100 meter sprint

She won Gold in the 200 meter race

She also won Gold in the 4x100 meter relay

In the same Olympics Florence Griffith Joyner won the Silver Medal in the 4x400 meter relay race.

After the 1988 Olympics Joyner unexpectedly announced her retirement from Track.

In 1995 Florence Griffith Joyner was inducted into the Olympics Hall of Fame with the first group of Olympic Stars that were inducted.

On this day in Sports History, July 1, 1961, Fredrick Carlton Lewis was born in Birmingham Alabama.

Carl Lewis has an amazing history in track and field, he does not only have a great Olympics history, he has a great record in Major International Competition as well.

Highlights of Carl Lewis's track career at the Olympics and other international competitions.

In the World Championships in1983 held in Helsinki; He won Gold in the 100 meter race.

He won the Gold Medal in the Long Jump

And Lewis won Gold in the 4x100 meter Relay.

In the World Championship in 1987 held in Rome; Carl Lewis won the Gold Medal in the 4x100 meter Relay

He won the Gold Medal in the 100 meter race

He also won the Gold in the Long Jump.

In the World Championships in 1991 held in Tokyo Carl Lewis won the Gold Medal in the 100 meter Race

Lewis won the Gold Medal in the 4x100 meter Relay

Lewis won the Silver Medal In the Long Jump in Tokyo

In the World Championships in 1993 Held in Stuttgart Carl Lewis won the Bronze Medal in the 200 meter race.

In the Pan American Games in 1979 held in San Juan P.R. Carl Lewis won the Bronze Med in the Long Jump

---

Ray G. Claveran

In the Pan American games in, 1987 held in Indianapolis Carl Lewis won the Gold Medal in the 4x100 meter Relay.

In the same Pan Am Games Carl Lewis won the gold in the Long Jump

In the Goodwill games in 1986 held in Moscow Russia Carl Lewis won the gold Medal in the 4x100 meter Relay

In the same Goodwill Games Lewis won the Bronze Medal in the 100 meter race.

In the goodwill games in 1990, held in Seattle Washington Carl Lewis won Gold in the Long Jump

In the same Goodwill Games in Seattle Lewis won the Silver Medal in the 100 meter sprint.

In the Goodwill games in 1994, held in St. Petersburg, Carl Lewis won the Gold Medal in the 4x100 meter Relay

Carl Lewis's Olympic record

In the 1984 Olympics held in Los Angeles California

Carl Lewis won the Gold Medal in the 100 meter race

Carl Lewis won the Gold Medal in the 200 meter race

He won the Gold in the 4x100 meter relay And in these same Olympics Carl Lewis won the Gold Medal in the Long Hump

In the 1988 Olympics held in Seoul Korea Carl Lewis won the Gold Medal in the 100 meter race

And in the same Olympics Lewis won the Gold Medal in the Long Jump and the Silver Medal in the 200 meter race

In the 1992 Olympics held in Barcelona Spain. Carl Lewis won the Gold Medal in the Long Jump

He also won the Gold Medal in the 4x100 meter relay

In the 1996 Olympics held in Atlanta Georgia; which was to become the last Olympics for this Legend in Track and Field, Carl Lewis won the Gold Medal in the Long Jump

Carl Lewis's medal count at the Olympics stands at 9 Gold and 1Silver

In the World Games his medal count is— 8 gold—1 Silver—1 bronze

In the Pan Am Games is medal count is—2 Gold —1 Bronze

In the Goodwill games his medal count is—3 Gold—1 Silver—1Bronze—For a total of 22 Gold—3 Silver—and 3 Bronze

Carl Lewis's illustrious career came to an end on August 26, 1997, following the 4x100 relay at the Berlin Grand Prix

In 2001Sports Illustrated named Carl Lewis the Olympian of the Century.

The International Olympic Committee named Lewis the Sportsman of the Century.

In the same year 2001 Carl Lewis was inducted into the USA Track and Field Hall of Fame

On this day in Sports History August 21, 1986, Usain St Leo Bolt was born in Sherwood Content, Jamaica, His residence is in Kingston Jamaica.

Usain Bolt, nicknamed Lightning Bolt is considered by many sportswriters and Track and Field fans as the greatest Track Star in

Ray G. Claveran

Olympic History. The lightning Bolt has won 23 first place finishes in major international events which includes the Olympics.

The events he excelled in are; the 100 meter, the 150 meters, the 200 meters, the 300, and the 400 meter races.

Highlights of Usain Bolt's Track career at the Olympics and other international competitions

In the World Junior Championships in 2002 held in Kingston Jamaica.

In the 200 meter Bolt won Gold

In the 4x100 meters relay Bolt won the Silver Medal

In the 4x400 relays Bolt won the Silver Medal

In the World Youth Championships in 2003 held in Sherbrooke

Usain Bolt won the Gold Medal in the 200 meter run.

The CARIFTA Games Junior(u,20) in 2003 held in Port of Spain.

In the 200 meter race Bolt won the Gold Medal

In the 400 meter race Bolt won the Gold Medal

The CAC Championships in 2005 held in Nassau

He won the Gold Medal in the 200meter race

The World Championships

The world Championships in 2007, held in Osaka Japan

Usain Bolt won the Silver in the 200 meter, and he won the Silver in the 4x100 meter relay.

The World Championships in 2009 held in Berlin Germany.

Usain Bolt won the Gold Medal in the 100 meter, the 200 meter and the 4x100 meter relay.

The World Championships in 2011 held in Daegu.

Usain Bolt won the Gold Medal in the 200 meter race and he won the Gold in the 4x100 meter relay

The World Championships in 2013 held in Moscow Russia Bolt won the Gold Medal in the 100 meter race and he won the Gold in the 200 meter Run and the 4x100 meter Relay

The World Championships in 2015, held in Beijing China Usain Bolt won the Gold in the 100 meter race, he won the 200 meter race and the Gold in the 4x100 meter relay

The World Championships in 2017, held in London England Usain Bolt won the Bronze medal in the 100 meter race.

In the World Relay Championships in 2015 held in Nassau

Bolts relay team won the Silver Medal in the 4x100 meter relay

There is much confusion about Jim Thorpe's date of birth, some biographies claim he was born in 1887, and some say he was born in 1888, some say May 22 others say May 28. His place of birth is also in dispute, but for sure he was born in Oklahoma. All I can say on the matter is: For the good of American Sports History I am glad he was born!!!

On this day in Sports History, March 28, 1953 the great Jim Thorpe died in Lomita California, at the age of 65.

The following are highlights of Jim Thorpe's career in the; Olympics, NFL Football, Major League Baseball, and Professional Basketball. (Surprised)?

Thorpe played in the Major Leagues for 7 years, six years with the New York Giants, In 1917 he played the first part of the season with the Cincinnati Reds and the last part of the season back with the Giants, Thorpe played 1 year with Boston Braves. He made his debut on April 14th 1913, and his final game was with Boston on September 25, 1919

Jim Thorpe's Major League Baseball statistics

His Batting average was—252
Home Runs—7—
Runs Batted in—82—Hits—176

Jim Thorpe's NFL football career

Jim Thorpe started his professional football career in 1913, one year after his Gold Medal wins in the 1912 Olympics. He played for the Indiana Based Pine Village Pros that played against local teams. In 1915 he signed with the Canton Bulldogs for $250 a game, ($5,919 today), which was a huge wage at that time. Before Thorpe signed with the Canton bulldogs they were averaging 1,200 fans a game, in Thorpe's first game for Canton 8,000 folks came to the game against the Massillon Tigers. With Thorpe in the line-up Canton won the title in 1916—1917—and in 1919.

In 1920 the Canton Bulldogs and 13 other professional football teams formed the APFA, the American Professional Football Association, two years later it would become the NFL, the National Football League.

IN 1923 Jim Thorpe was selected for the Green Bay Press Gazette's first All- NFL team.

From 1920-1921Thorpe was nominally the first President of the American Professional Football Association (APFA).

Thorpe received many honors and for his athletic accomplishments in the sports world.

The Associated Press named Jim Thorpe the greatest athlete for the first 50 year of the 20th century.

In Pennsylvania a town was named in his honor and a monument site in the town there is the site of his remains.

In 1951 Jim Thorpe was portrayed in the Movie Jim Thorpe- All American.

Thorpe played in 52 NFL game for six teams from 1920-1928

Jim Thorpe retired fro football at the age of 41.

Jim Thorpe was inducted into the Professional Football Hall of Fame as part of the inaugural class 1963

Jim Thorpe's Professional Basketball career

In 1925 Jim Thorpe was the main feature of the of the "World Famous Indians" of La Rue traveling basketball team, "Jim Thorpe's World Famous Indians barnstormed for about 3 years. The main reason most people were unaware that he played professional basketball was because it was not well documented at the time. It was not until 2005 that it was discovered in an old book that documented his time in Professional Basketball

Jim Thorpe's Olympics Career

Jim Thorpe participated in only one Olympics; the 1912 Olympics games in Stockholm Sweden, and they soon became one of the most famous

Olympics of all time. After the games, as was accustoms at the time, the medals were awarded during the closing ceremonies of the games. Jim Thorpe won two Gold Medals, one for the Pentathlon, presented by Czar Nichols the 2nd of Russia and one for the, Decathlon presented by King Gustav v of Sweden, some sources recount that King Gustav said to Jim Thorpe, "You sir are the greatest athlete in the world."

Thorpe was stripped of his two Gold Medals after it was found out that he had played in two seasons of semi pro baseball. In 1983 the International Olympic Committee restored Jim Thorpe's Olympic Medals; 30 years after he passed away.

A few honors earned by one of the greatest athletes in sports history

In Pennsylvania there is a city named after Jim Thorpe; in the city of Jim Thorpe there is a monument featuring the Quote from King Gustav; ("You sir are the greatest athlete in the world"). His grave rests on mounds of soil brought in from his native state of Oklahoma, and soil from the stadium that he won his Olympic gold Medals in.(WOW)

In 1950; the Associated press took two polls of about 350-400 sportswriters and broadcasters in the first poll they voted Jim Thorpe the greatest athlete in the first half of the 20th century. In the second poll they voted Jim Thorpe the "greatest American Football Player" of the first half century.

In1999; the Associated Press voted Jim Thorpe in third place after Babe Ruth and Michael Jordan as the best athlete of the 20th century.

President Richard Nixon, as authorized by U.S. Senate Joint Resolution 73 proclaimed April 16, as "Jim Thorpe day" to promote the nationwide recognition of Jim Thorpe.

In 1986 the Jim Thorpe Association established the Jim Thorpe Award given every year to the best defensive back in College Football.

On February 3rd, 1998 the U. S. Postal service issued a 32 cent stamp honoring Thorpe as part of the Celebrate the Century stamp sheet series.

ABC Sports conducted a poll of sports fans and the fans voted Jim Thorpe the Greatest Athlete of the Twentieth Century Thorpe won this honor over such legends as Ruth, Ali, Owens, Gretzky, Jack Nicklaus and Michael Jordan.

Jim Thorpe in inducted into 4 Halls of Fame

Jim Thorpe was inducted into the Pro Football Hall of Fame in 1963 he was one of seven player inducted in the first class. Thorpe was also inducted into the halls of Fame for College Football, American Olympics, and the National Track and Field Competition.

CHAPTER 15

● ●

THIS DAY IN SPORTS HISTORY IN TENNIS

In Tennis when you read about a tennis player that has set a record or competeted in an event in the Open Era: this means that after 1968 all major Tennis Tournaments were open to Professional tennis player as well as amateurs. Befor 1968 only amateurs were allowed to compete in Grand Slam Tournaments and other tournaments that were sanctioned by the ILTF this includes the Davis Cup

On this day in Sports History, August 14, 2011 Serena Williams won the Rogers Cup Tennis Tournament defeating Samantha Stosur of Australia

On this day in Sports History September 8, 1968, Arthur Ashe won the U.S. Open Singles Title at Forrest Hills, New York. Ashe remains the only African American to win a man's title at the U.S., Open, The Australian Open and Wimbledon. It is believed Ashe contracted HIV from a tainted blood transfusion Arthur Ashe died from Aids related Pneumonia in 1993

On this day in Sports History, September 8,2018, Naomi Osaka Defeated her long time idol, Serena Williams to become the first player from Japan to win a major tennis title .

On this day in Sports History July 15,2018 Angelique Kerber from Germany, Defeated American Super-Star Serena William, 6--3 6--3 to win the women's Finals at Wimbledon

On this day in Sports History July 13,2018, Kevin Anderson from South Africa defeated American, John Isner in the Wimbledon Semi Finals in the second longest match at Wimbledon, the match lasted 6 ½ Hours

CHAPTER 16

● ●

A FEW LEGENDS IN TENNIS

On this day in Sports History, October 18, 1956 Martina Navratilova was born in Prague Czechoslavakia.
In 1981 Martina Navratilova became an American citizen and her residence is in Miami, Florida

On September 6, 2014 Martina proposed to her long time girl friend Julia Lemigova at the U.S. Open, They were Married on December 15, 2014 in New York

Navratalova turned professional in 1975, and retired in 2006.Tennis Magazine selected Martina as the greatest female tennis star for the years ;1975-2005 Today she is considered by many experts in the Tennis World as the greatest female tennis player of all time.

Because of her concern for animal rights and her involement in under privleged children charities, she is one of my very favorite atletes in the world .I wish her a happy and wonderful life.

High-lights of Martina Navratilova Tennis Career

Navratilova held the number one ranking for for both singles and doubles for more than 200 weeks. She holds the record for holding the singles number one spot for 332 weeks,and the doubles for over 200 weeks.—she won the Wimbledon Title in singles 9 times.—She won 18 Grand Slam titles and 31Major womens doubles titles. Which is an all-time record,.Martina also won 10 major mixed doubles titles. Martina Navratilova has won more Grand Slam titles, male or female than any other tinnis player in the History of the Game.

Martina's career record in singles 1442–219—86.8 %

Her Grand Slam singles include —

The Australian Open Martina won in 1981— 1983 — 1985

The French Open she won in—1982— 1984

Wimbledon—Navratilova won in 1978—1979—1982—1983—1984— 1985—1986—1987—1990— (A record 9 times)

The U.S. Open—she won—1983—1984—1986—1987—

Martina Navratilova won the Tour Finals —1978—1979—1981— 1983—1984—1985—1986 in March—1986 Nov.

⟨ᗰᗰᗷ⟩

In Doubles her career record 747—143

Grand Slam doubles include—The Australian Open—she won in—1980—1982—1983—1984—1985—1987—1988—1989

The French open She won in— 1975— 1982—1984—1985—1986— 1987—1988—(5 times in a row)

Wimbledon— Martina and partner won in—1976—979—1981—1982—1983—1984—1986—

U. S. Open— She won in— 1977—1978—1980—1983—1984—1986— 1987—1989—1990

Tour Finals she won in—1980—1981--1982—1983—1984—1985—1986- Nov. —1987—1988—1989—1991—

Grand SlamMixed Doubles

Australian Open—Won in 2003

Frenc Open won in 1974—1985

Wimbledon She won in 1985—1993—1995—2003

U.S. Open she won in 1985—1987—2006—

Team competitions

Fed Cup—she won in- 1975—1982—1986—1989

On this day in Sports HistorySeptember 26, 1981 Serena Jameka Williams was born in Saginaw Michigan

Serena Williams is one of the top 2 or 3 greatest female Tennis players of all time.

High-lights of Serena Williams Tennis career

Serena williams reached the world number one rating in womens Tennis on July 8th,2002; williams was rankd number one on eight seperate occasions, the 6th time she was ranked number one, she kept the rating for 186 consecutive weeks, this tied her for the record that was held by Steffi Graf—Serena held the number one ranking for a total of 319 weeks, wich ranks third behind Steffi Graf and Martina Navratilova

At the age of 37 Serena is ranked at number 16 in the world and still going strong.

Willams career record stands at 801–136 =85.49 5

Serena has won 72 WTA Titles—5th in over-all rankings.

Grand Slam Singles

The Australian Open—Williams won the title in 2003—2005—2007—2009—2010—2015—2017

French Open—williams won the title in—2002—2013—2015—

Wimbledon—Serena won the title in—2002—2003—2009—2010—2012—2015—2016

U.S. Open—Serena won the title in—1999—2002—2008—2012—2013—2014—

Other Tournaments

Grand Slam Cup—Williams won the title in—1999

Tour Finals —Serena williams won the title in—2001—2009—2012—2013—2014—

Doubles —Career record—187—33 =85%

Grand Slam Doubles

Australian Open—Williams and partner won the title in—2001—2003—2009—2010—

French Open—Serena Williams And partner won the title in—1999—2010

Wimbledon—Williams won the title in—2000—2002—2008—2009—2012—2016—

U.S. Open—Serena and partner won the title in—1999—2009

Grand Slam Mixed Doubles

Australian Open—Williams —2nd place in 1999

French Open—Williams— 2nd place in 1999

Wimbledon—Williams won the title in—1998

U.S. Open— Serena and partner won the title in 1998

Team Competitions

Fed Cup—Won title in 1999 with a record of 16–1

Hopman Cup—Won title in 2003—2008

Olympic Medal Record

2000 Sydney Olympic games Representing the U.S.Selena and partner won Gold —in Doubles

2008 Beijing Olympic games Selena and Partner won gold in Doubles

2012 London Olympic Games Serena Williams won Gold in singles Matches

2012 London games Williams and partner won Gold in the Doubles Matches

On this day in Sports History August 8, 1981, Roger Federer was born in Basel Switzerland.

Highlights of Roger Federer 's career in Tennis

At the age of 38 Roger Federer in June 15,2018 was ranked 2nd in the world rankings by the ATP. Roger Federer held the Number One Ranking by the ATP for 310 weeks which includes at one point a consecutive streak of 237 weeks. All-time

Roger Federer turned professional in1998, and has since has establised himself as one of the greatest tennis players of all time

At Wimbledon he has won the mens singles championship a record eight times —A joint record of six Australian Opens— a record of five consecutive U.S. Opens.—and one French Open. The Grand Slam in Tennis is ; the Australian Open—the French Open—Wimbledon and the U.S. Open in a Calender Year,Steffi Graf is the only tennis player,man or woman to acieve the Grand Slam.in 1988 she won the Australian the French Open, Wimbledon and the U.S. open And she won the Gold Medal in the Olympics that same year….. Roger Federer is just one of eight men that have achieved a career Grand Slam. The other seven are:

Don budge in 1937-1938
Fred Perry in 1933-1936
Rod Laver in 1960–1969
Roy Emerson in 1961–1967
Andre Agassi in 1992–2003
Rafeal Nadel in 2005–2018
Novak Djokovic in 2008—2018
Roger Federer achieved his Career Grand Slam in 2003–2006.

Singles career record

Federer has won 1168 and lost 256 =82.02%

He has 98 career titles 2nd in the Open Era

Grand Slam Singles

Australia Open—Federer won the title in—2004—2006—2007—2010 —2017—2018—

French Open —he won the title in 2009

Wiimbledon —Federer won the title in—2003—2004—2005— 2006—2007—2009—2012—2017—(Should have changed the name of tournament to the Roger Federer Open!)

U.S. Open Roger Federer won the title in—2004—2005—2006—2007 —2008—(Really???

Men that have won at least 10 grand slams

Roger Federer has won 20 grand slam Tournaments singles

Rafeal Nadalhas won 17

Pete Sampras has won 14

NovakDjokovic has won 14

Roy Emerson has won 12

Rod Laver has won 11

Bjorn Borg has won 11

Bill Tildon has won 10—(There is a Golf Corse in Oakland California named after Mr. Tildon—Tildon Park).

Other Tournaments

Tour Finals,he won the title in—2003—2004—2006—2007—2010—2011

2012 London Olympic Games Federer won the Silver Medal

Doubles Record

Career record 129—89=59%

Titles— Federer has won— 8 Doubles titles

Grand Slam Doubles

Australian Open in 2003—Federer and partner were 3rd

French Open in 2000—lost in first round

Wimbledon in 2000 Qf

U.S. Open Roger Federer and Partner lost in the 3rd round

Other Doubles tournaments

Beijing Olympic Games in 2008—Federer and Partner won the Gold

Team Competitions

Davis Cup—In 2014 the team won the title

Hopman Cup the team won the title in—2001—2018

On this day in Sports History June,6,1956 Bjorn Rune Borg was born in Stockholm Sweden

Borg turned professional in 1973 and retired in 1983 at the age of 26.

In his short career he still managed to become one of the greatest tennis players of all-time,.In 1979 Borg became the first tennis player to win over one million dollars in prize money, he also made millions in endorsements throughout his career.

Highlights of Bjorn Borg's career inb Tennis

Singles record

Borg won a total of 639 singles Matches and lost only 130 which is an 83.09 winning percentage

He has 64 career Titles to his name

Grand Slam Singles record

Australian Open in 1974—lost in 3rd round

French Open —Bjorn Borg won the Title in—1974—1975—1978—1979—1980— 1981 (4 in a row)

Wimbledon —Borg won the title in—1976—1977— 1978—1979—1980 (5 in a row)

U.S. Open —Bjorn Borg won the title in—1976—1978—1980—1981

Other Tournaments

Tour Finals Borg won the title in —1979—1980

WCT Finals-Borg won the title in—1976

Doubles Record

Borgs Career record in Doubles stands at 86–81 which comes to a 51.2 per cent win record

Borg has 4 career titles

Grand Slam doubles results

Australian Open 1973—lost in 3rd round

French Open 1974—1975—Lost in semi finals

Wimbledon 1976—Lost in 3rd round

U.S. Open 1975—Loastin 3rd Round

Team Competitions

Davis Cup The team won title in—1975

On this Day in Sports History, June 14, 1969, Stefanie Maria Graf was born in Mannheim Weast Germany, Her residence is in Las Vegas Nevada .(A very good Place to spend her fortune from Tennis)

Steffi Graf turned professional in October 18, 1982 and retired in August 13,1999

Highlights of Steffi Graf's career in tennis

Steffi Graf Steffi Graf was rankedthe world number one By the WTA for a Record 377 toyal weeks. No other tennis player has held that honor as long Male or Female.

Steffi has won 107 Singles Titles which pus her in 3ʳᵈ place behind Martina Navratilova with 167 titles and another great female tennis star Chris Evert with 157

Singles

Steffi Graf's Career record Stands at—900—115 = 88.67%

!07 singles Titles

Steffi Graf acieves the Golden Slam

In 1988 Steffi Graf became the only Tennis Player male or female to win the Australian Open—The French Open—Wimbledon—and the U.S. Open all in the same year. Wow

To win all four Major Tournament sin the Same year is one of the greatest acievements in Sports History...

Grand Slam Singles

Australian Open—Graf won the title in—1988—1989—1990—1994

French Open—Graf won the title in—1987—1988—1993—1995—1996—1999—

Wimbledon—Graf won the title in—1988—1989—1991—1992—1993—1995—1996—

The U.S. Open Steffi Graf won the title in—1988—1989—1993—1995—1996—

Other Tournaments

Tour Finals Steffi Graf won the title in 1987—1989—1993—1995—1996—

Olympic Games—Graf won the Gold in 1988--

Doubles— Her record stands at 173-72

She has 11 Career titles

Grand Slam Doubles

Australian Open Graf and partner—SF-1988—1989

French Open—Graf and partner—f-1986—1987—1989

Wimbledon Steffi Fraf and partner won the title in—1988

U.S. Open—SF in 1986—1987—1988—1989

Grand Slam Mixed Doubles

Australian OpenGraf and partner lost in 2nd round— 1991

French Open Graf and Partner lost in 2nd round-1994

Wimbledon Graf and partner lostin thesemi finalsU.S. Open Graf and partner lost in 1st roud in1994

Team Competition

Fed Cup—Team won in—1987—1992—

Hopman Cup—Team won in —1993

● ● ● ● ● ● ● ● ● ● ● ● ● ● ● ● ● ● ●

CHAPTER 17

ON THIS DAY IN SPORTS HISTORY IN OTHER SPORTS

On this day in Sports History January 6, 1994 American figure skater Nancy Kerrigan was hit on the leg by an assailant at the Cobo Arens in Detroit City. Four men -which included Jeff Gillooly, the former husband of Nancy Kerrigans rival, Tonya Harding. They were later sentenced to prison for their Part in the attack. Tonya Harding denied that she knew about the attack. Tonya later was placed on probation after she pleaded guilty to conspiracyto hinder prosecution.

On this day in Sports History,Sunday January 13, 2019, Marcel Hirscherwon the World Cup Slalom and set a man's record for the most wins by one skier in at a single venue It was his ninth career win at ADELBODEN Switzerland.

On this day in Sports History January 9, 2006, Joannie Rochette, from Canada won the second of six consecutive Canadian Championship titles. Rochette represented Canada in the 2006 Winter Olympics in Turin and the 2010 Winter Olympics in Vancouver Canada. During a practice session, Joannie Rochette received the news that her Mother had died shortly after arriving in Vancouver to watch Joannie participate in the Olympics, Rochette won the Bronze Medal, and dedicating her medal win to her mom. Following her win she was awarded the Terry Fox Award for showing courage in the face of adversity.

On this day in Sports History March 11, 1993 Kurt Browning won his fourth World Figure Skating Championship Title

On this day in Sports History March 15, 2013 Patrick Chan of Canada won his third consecutive World Figure Skating Title. Chan was the first man in 13 years to win three strait men's single figure skating titles.

On this day in Sports History March 6, 1954, Roger Bannister, a medicalstudent from Great Britain became the first person to run the Mile in Less than 4 minutes, His time was 59.4 seconds.

On this day in Sports History April 19, 1897, The Boston Marathon was held for the first time. John Mc Dermot was the winner in the time of 2 hours 55 minutes and 10 seconds.

On this day in Sports History July 15, 2018, France wins the World Cup over Croatia 4--2

On this day in Sports History, December 31,1967 Evel Kn ievel attempted to jump the Fountains at Caesars Palace in Las Vegas, he did not make the jump and Knievel ended up with a concussion, broken ribs, a crushed pelvis and femur, fractures to his wrist and both ankles.

On this day in Sports History, March 5, 1982 Steve Podborski won the World Cup Mens Downhill Skiing Championship, he won the title with three wins and two second place finishes in the ten race event Podbroski became the first North American to win the Title. Steve Podbroski is from Toronto Canada. Later that year he was made an officer of the Order of Canada

On this day in Sports History, August 16, 1974 Sixteen year old Cindy Nicholas of Toronto Canada Swam Lake Ontario in 15 hours and eighteen minutes, She broke the record by almost 3 hours.

The following year on July 30th 1975, Cindy Nicholas, now 17 years old set the women's record for swimming the English Channel in 9 hours and 46 minutes.

On this day in Sports History, August 7, 1987, Vicki Keith a 26 year old Marathon swimmer and swimming instructor from Kingston Ontario, Canada, completed the first double crossing of Lake Ontario in 56 hours. She estimated that she lost 40 pound During the 56 hour swim.

Marilyn Bell was the first to complete the one way crossing of Lake Ontario in 1954

On this day in Sports History, December 22, 1993, Gabriel Medina was born in Sao Paulo, Brazil. Medina became a Surfing sensation at a very young age, in 2009 at 15 years of age Medina turned professional. He won the Maresia Surf International. He broke a long standing record and became the youngest male to win a professional surfing event.

In 2014 Medina won the Quicksilver Pro Gold Coast Competition and 2 more events to win the over-all 2014 ASP World Championship. Gabriel Medina is the only surfer credited to have landed a back-flip in professional competition. In 2015 He became the first Brazilian to win the Hawaiian Triple Crown of Surfing.

On this day in Sports History, October 31, 2003, Bethany Hamilton, a teen-aged surfer was attacked by a shark while surfing with friends off the coast of Kauai, Hawaii; she lost her arm just below the left shoulder. Within a month of the attack, Bethany returned to competitive surfing and in 2004 she was awarded the ESPY Award for the Best Comeback Athlete, as well as the Teen Choice Award of courage.

On this day in Sports History May 30th 1911, Ray Harroun won the first ever Indianapolis 500 car race. The average speed of the first winner was 74.4 miles per hour.

On this day in Sports History September 3, 1935 Sir Malcolm Campbell at the Bonneville Salt Flats broke his own land speed record and was the first man to break the 300 M. P H. barrier driving the Campbell-Railton Blue Bird. Campbell modified his vehicle adding a powerful 2300 horsepower supercharged Roll- Royce V-12 engine, and double tires to the rear, for better traction.

On this day in Sports History, April 20, 2008, Danica Patrick, won the Indy Japan 300 in her 50th career start and became the first female winner in Indy Car history

On this day in Sports History, May 22, 1977 Janet Guthrie became the first woman to qualify for the Indianapolis 500 auto race

On this day in Sports History May 28, 1995, Jacques Villeneuve won the Indianapolis 500 and became the first Canadian of the Indy-500.

ON this day in Sports History November 15th, 1992, Richard Petty in his famous Number 43 raced his final race at the Hooters 500 in NASCAR's Winston Series. Petty's career spanned more than 35 year. Petty won the Daytona 500 seven times. Petty was highly loved and respected by most competitors and fans alike. After his final race Petty circled the track one more time to wave to the 160,000 plus fans that were in attendance

On this day in Sports History, January 17, 2013 Lance Armstrong an American Cyclist who had won 7 Tour de France titles confessed to using performance enhancing drugs in a TV interview while on the Oprah Winfrey show. In 2012 a year prior to his admission of using the banned substance the U.S. anti-doping held an investigation and concluded Lance Armstrong had used the banned substances throughout his cycling career, he was banned for life from competition, and was stripped of his 7 Tour de France Titles. Armstrong lost most of his sponsors, removed from the charity he founded over his conduct.

We all make mistakes in life myself I feel for this man, remember what a great man once said; (he who is without sin cast the first stone).

On this day in Sports History, June 9th, 2018, Justify ridden by 52 year old Jokey Mike Smith becomes a legend in Sport History by winning the 150th running of the Belmont Stakes to become the13[th] Triple Crown winner.

On this day in Sports History, September 2, 2013, Diana Nyad became the first person to swim the From Cuba to the United States, she accomplished the feat without the aid of a shark case. The 177-kilometer swim took her 53 hours, what is amazing is the fact that Diana was 64 at the time, Diana Nyad had attempted the swim 4 time befor.

● ● ● ● ● ● ● ● ● ● ● ● ● ● ● ● ● ● ●

CHAPTER 18

A FEW LEGENDS IN OTHER SPORTS

On this day in Sports HistoryOctober 23, 1940, Edson Arentes Do Nasimento was born inTresCoracoes Brazil. Later in life he became a very famouse soccer player known as Pele. Pele is considered by many Sports writers, Fans and many professional soccer players as the greatest player of all time. Pele, also known as the Black Pearl was one of a few men in sports that became as popular after his prime as he was in his prime.

Pele was only 15 years old when he started playing for Santos, and only 16 when he played for the Brazil National Team.

Highlights of Pele's Career in soccer

From 1956—1974 Pele played 638 games and scored 619 goals playing for Santos

From 1975 —1977 Pele played 56 games and scored 31 goals Playing for The New York Cosmos

for a total of 694 games and a total of 650 goals, plus 92 games and 77 goals for the brazilian National Team for a grand total of 786 games and 727 goals.

__The 77 goals makes Pele the All-time Leading scorer for the Brazilian National Team__

FIFA World Cup

The National Team won the Gold in Sweden in 1958

The national Team won the Gold in Chile in 1962

The National Team won the Gold in Mexico in 1970— **Pele is the only player to have won 3 FIFA World Cups**

Copa America

The National Team won the Silver medal in Argentina in 1959

Onthis day in Sports History July2, 1937 Richard Lee Petty was born in Level Cross,Randolph County North Carolina.

Richard Petty's father Lee Petty was also a NASCAR driver

Highlights of Richard Petty's career in NASCAR

Petty started his NASCAR career in July 18,1958 at the age of 21, His first race was in Toronto Ontario, Canada. In 1959 Richard Petty was named Rookie of the Year because of his nine top ten finishes, which included six top five finiishes.

In 1963 Petty won his first race, but his father Lee Petty protested complaining of a scoring error by the officials and a few hours later his father. Lee Petty was awarded the win.

In 1959 Richard Petty was the Grand National Series Rookie of the Year.

Grand National Series Champion from—1964—1967—

Winsto Cup Series Champion—1971—1972—1974—1975—and 1979

Daytona 500 Petty won the race in—1981

The Southern 500 Petty won the race in—1967

The worlld 600 Petty won the race in—1975—19777

Petty was the all-time wins leader in Sprint Cup Series —200 wins

All-time Poles leader in Sprint Cup Series—123

Richard Petty holds the record for the most Sprint Cup Series win in a single season—27 wins in—1967

Petty holds the record for the most consecutive Sprint Cup Series wins—He won 10 times in —1967

Petty owns the record for the most all-time wins at the Daytona International Speedway—he has won there 10 times.

Richard Petty was voted the most popular NASCAR'S Driver in—1962—1964—1968—1974—1975—1976—1977—and 1978

Petty was inducted into the Motorsports Hall of Fame of America in—1989

He was inducted into the International Motorsports Hall of Fame in—1997

Petty was awarded the Medal of Freedom in—1962 Richard Petty was named one of NASCAR'S 50 Greatest Drivers in—1998

Petty was inducted into theDiecast Hall of Fame in—2011

Richard Lee Petty was inducted into The NASCAR Hall of Fame in—2010

On this day in Sports Jistory, April 29,1951, Ralph Dale Earnhardt was born in Kannapolis, North Carolina was born.

On this day in Sports History Earnhardt died on February 18,2001 at Daytona Beach Florida,

Earnhardt died because of an accident while in a car race at the daytona beach Speedway He was only 49 years old.

Highlights of Dale Earnhardt Career in Autosports

Winston Cup Series Champion—1980—1986—1987—1990—1991—1993—1994—

Iroc Champion—1990—1995—1999—2000—

The Daytona 500 Earnhardt won the title in —1998

The Southern 500 Earnhardt won the title in—1987—1989—1990

The Brickyard 400 Earnhardt won in1995

The Coca-Cola 600 Dale Earnhardt won the race in—1986—1992—1993

The Winston 500 Earnhardt won in 1990—1994—1999—2000

Earnhardt won the Winston in —1987—1990—1993

Led Winston Cup Series in wins—1987—1990

Led Winston Cup Series in poles in—1990

Earnhardt was the winner of the first Budweiser Late Model Sportsmans Series Race in—1982

Led Busch Series in Wins in—1986—

In 1979 Dale Earnhardt was named Winston Cup Series Rookie of the year.

In 2001 Dale Earnhardt was voted Winston Cup Series Most Popular Driver (posthumously)

In 1998 Dale Earnhardt was named as one of NASCAR's 50 Greatest Drivers

IN 2002 Ralph Dale Earnhardt wa inducted into the Motorsports Hall of Fame

In 2006 Ralph Dale Earnhardt wa inducted into the International Motorsports Hall of Fame

In 2010 Ralph Dale Earnhardt was inducted int The NASCAR Hall of Fame

CPSIA information can be obtained
at www.ICGtesting.com
Printed in the USA
BVHW031122180319
542953BV00031B/314/P